THE HOLY SPIRIT

in Biblical and Pastoral Perspective

J. W. Rogerson

BEAUCHIEF
ABBEY·PRESS

Published by Beauchief Abbey Press.

Copyright © J W Rogerson, 2013

ISBN 978-0-9576841-0-2

A CIP catalogue record for this title is available from the British Library.

CONTENTS

INTRODUCTION

Two years ago I ventured to write a book on the subject of prayer, one of my reasons being that I did not consider myself to be very good at it, and thought that a book by a non-expert might help other non-experts.[1] In the event, I have been much encouraged by the reviews, as well as by personal communications expressing gratitude for what I wrote. It is for a similar reason that I have now ventured to write a book on the Holy Spirit. Although it is a subject about which I have read a great deal over the years, I am not a 'charismatic' Christian and do not consider myself to be very good at the practice of the Holy Spirit (whatever that is). I would like to think that what I have written will encourage other non-charismatic Christians and congregations to think more deeply about the Holy Spirit and to discover in new ways his presence among them. Like the work on prayer, some of the material in the present book originates from sermons preached at Beauchief Abbey, in this case during 2012. I am grateful to the congregation for being willing to listen to my explorations.

Readers and reviewers will notice that I have made many references to publications by the late C. K. Barrett, who died in August 2011. During my time in Durham, from 1964 to 1979, I attended Barrett's New Testament Seminar every week that it was held, and learned an enormous amount

---

[1] J. W. Rogerson, *The Art of Biblical Prayer*, London: SPCK, 2011.

about the New Testament. My many and deliberate references to his work are my way of trying to show my appreciation for his friendship, and his example of scholarship of the highest quality. My wife, Rosalind, has again typed the manuscript from my longhand, a labour of love that is again much appreciated.

CHAPTER 1

Confusions and Difficulties

Language about the Holy Spirit in church worship is confused and contradictory. On the one hand the Holy Spirit is said to be a 'person' of the Trinity and it is not unknown for clergy to rebuke members of their congregations for calling the Holy Spirit 'it' rather than 'he'.[2] On the other hand the church speaks of the Holy Spirit as a gift, or as 'indwelling' believers. How can this be so if the Holy Spirit is in some sense a 'person'? Each matter will be dealt with in turn.

There are Christian hymns that are addressed to the Holy Spirit as a 'person' of the Trinity. The well-known and ancient hymn Veni, Creator Spiritus, 'Come, Holy Ghost, our

---

[2] The use of the word 'he' in this book for the Holy Spirit is a matter of grammatical usage and has no gender implications.

souls inspire' is used at Ordinations in the Church of England, and there are similar hymns that ask the Holy Spirit to 'come' to worshippers or persons being admitted to special offices in the church.[3] Prayers addressed to the Holy Spirit are rare (as are prayers addressed to Jesus) but here is one:

> O Holy Spirit of life, who fillest all the world, we worship and adore thee. Spirit of light, who teachest all truth, we worship and adore thee. Source of all gifts of nature and of grace, of knowledge natural and supernatural, we worship and adore thee. For that thou hast made and endowed us, taught and reproved us, borne with us, recovered us, restored us; Lord and lifegiver, we worship and adore thee.[4]

There is, however, language about the Holy Spirit which is *impersonal*. The introduction to the Confirmation service of the Book of Common Prayer as proposed in 1928, after quoting from Acts 8.4-6, 12, 14-17 goes on to assert that

> The Scripture here teacheth us that a special gift of the Holy Spirit is bestowed through laying on of hands with prayer.

The passage from Acts has related how Peter and John were sent from Jerusalem to Samaria to lay hands on believers who had been baptised in the name of the Lord Jesus, but who had not yet 'received' the Holy Spirit. This defect is remedied by Peter and John. In the proposed 1928 service the prayer that accompanies the laying on of hands by the bishop repeats one from 1662, asking for a 'daily increase' in the Holy Spirit rather than a bestowal. A bestowal is, however, envisaged in the Alternative Service Book of 1980: 'Let your Holy Spirit rest upon *them*' (the candidates for confir-

---

[3] The word 'ghost' is an ancient Germanic word for 'spirit', similar to the German 'Geist'.

[4] *New Every Morning*, London: British Broadcasting Corporation, 1936, p.97.

mation) says the bishop, prior to the laying on of hands. The prayer that accompanies the laying on of the bishop's hands is

Confirm, O Lord, your servant N with your Holy Spirit.

The idea that the Holy Spirit is a kind of power, or influence, is found in the prayers for the Royal Family at Morning and Evening Prayer in the 1662 Prayer Book. The phrases 'replenish him with the grace of thy Holy Spirit' and 'endue them with thy Holy Spirit' are found. In the Occasional Prayers of the proposed 1928 Prayer Book, God is asked to 'pour thy Spirit upon thy Church'. He is said to have consecrated the first day of the week to be a day of rest 'through thy Spirit in the Church'. Candidates preparing for Confirmation are said to be 'seeking the gift of the Holy Spirit', while the guidance of the Holy Spirit is sought for sessions of the National Assembly of the Church of England (the forerunner of the General Synod). There are also prayers that imply that the Holy Spirit in some sense 'dwells' in believers and the church. The 1980 Collect for Pentecost 4 thanks God for sending 'the Spirit of your Son into our hearts' while a prayer in *New Every Morning* affirms that God has taught us in his holy Word 'that our bodies are temples of thy Spirit'.

A first reaction to the statements about the Holy Spirit as a 'person' or as power or influence is that they cannot all be right. If the Holy Spirit is a 'person' of the Trinity, how can he be 'conveyed' by the laying on of hands of a bishop or anyone else; and does not this make the Holy Spirit an object that certain humans can control, and therefore an object less than God? In what sense can a 'person' be said to 'dwell' in someone's heart? In what sense can someone be or become a temple for the Holy Spirit? In the next chapter an attempt will be made to find a way of thinking and speaking about the Holy Spirit as part of the Trinity that will also make sense of the language about 'dwelling' and being bestowed. For the moment this chapter will try to explain *how* the apparent confusion and contradiction came about.

The evidence of the New Testament

The uncertainty whether the Holy Spirit is a person or a force is already present in the New Testament, especially in the Acts of the Apostles. Acts 13.2 records that while the members of the church in Antioch were worshipping and fasting the Holy Spirit said, 'Separate me Barnabas and Saul for the work whereunto I have called them'. From the context it is likely that the Holy Spirit spoke through one of the prophets referred to in the preceding verse; but, as Barrett points out,[5] 'the Spirit sometimes speaks directly'. The references given by Barrett are interesting. In 8.29 the Spirit tells Philip to go to the Ethiopian's chariot. In 10.19 the Spirit tells Simon Peter that three men are looking for him (see also 11.12). At Acts 16.6-7 Paul and his companions are forbidden by the Holy Spirit to speak the word in Asia and are prevented by the Spirit of Jesus from going into Bithynia.

As over against these passages which emphasise the Holy Spirit as a person speaking to believers, there are the passages that represent him as a power, whose bestowal is in some cases indicated by those who receive it when they 'speak in tongues'.[6] Reference has been made above to the citation of parts of Acts 8 in the proposed 1928 Confirmation

---

[5] C.K. Barrett, *The Acts of the Apostles* (International Critical Commentary), vol.1 Acts I – XIV, Edinburgh: T. & T. Clark, 1994, p.605.

[6] The phenomenon of 'speaking in tongues' will be discussed later. See index.

service. What the excerpt omits is the fact that a disciple named Simon tries to bribe Peter into giving him the power to convey the Holy Spirit by the laying on of hands (Acts 8.18-20). We are a long way from the Holy Spirit as a person guiding the Christian missionaries. Another important passage is in Acts 10.44-7, where the Holy Spirit 'falls' (Greek *epepesen*) upon the family of Cornelius while Peter is preaching. The family is not yet baptised, and Peter commands that this should be done. There is no mention of laying on of hands. In Acts 19.1-7 Paul finds in Ephesus some believers who had received John the Baptist's baptism and had not heard of the Holy Spirit. Paul instructs and baptises them and lays hands upon them so that the Holy Spirit comes upon them.

In later chapters it will be necessary to deal in more detail with the Holy Spirit in the letters of Paul and the Gospel of John. For the moment it can be noted that the tension between 'person' and power can be found in these writings also. In Romans 8.15 Paul speaks of the Holy Spirit as something that his readers had *received*; but in 8.26 he says that the Spirit helps us in our weakness and intercedes on our behalf. In John chapters 14-16 Jesus describes the Holy Spirit as 'another Advocate' who will be sent by the Father in Jesus's name.[7] Against this, John 7.39 speaks of the Spirit, 'which they that believe on him should receive'. Outside Acts, Paul and John (the first three gospels will be considered in a later chapter) the letter to the Hebrews also displays the tension between the Holy Spirit as person and power. A quotation from Psalm 95.7-11 at Hebrews 3.7-22 is

---

[7] The translation 'Advocate' depends on the fact that the Greek word in John, *parakletos*, is a loan-word in Rabbinic Hebrew and Aramaic, *peraqlit*, meaning 'Advocate'. See also I John 2.1 'if any man sin, we have an advocate with the Father'.

prefaced by the words 'as the Holy Ghost saith' whereas Hebrews 6.4 says that believers have become 'partakers of the Holy Ghost'.

Developments in the history of the church

It would be easy to conclude from the above evidence that the church simply took up and developed the ambiguity of the New Testament on whether the Holy Spirit was a person or a power and influence; but this was not the case. Although the doctrine of the Trinity is implicit in the New Testament and needed to be elaborated in order for sense to be made of the revelation of God in Jesus Christ, this elaboration took time and generated many bitter arguments.[8] The main issue was that of the relation of the Father to the Son, and only when that was settled, in the 4th century, was the matter of the status of the Holy Spirit considered. Even after that, there were many discussions of the nature and mode of operation of the Holy Spirit over the centuries.

The lack of a clear resolution of the tension between the Holy Spirit as a person and as power (assuming that a resolution is possible or desirable) has led to outbreaks of enthusiasm for the Spirit in the course of church history. An early outbreak was Montanism, that began around AD 172.[9] Led by a man named Montanus it also featured two prophetesses named Priscilla and Quintilla, and became a sufficiently serious manifestation of Christianity to claim the allegiance of the important Christian apologist Tertullian, around AD 207/8. In the nineteenth century a new outbreak of Spirit-centred enthusiasm led to the founding of the

---

[8] See J.N.D. Kelly, *Early Christian Doctrines*, London: A. & C. Black, 1958.

[9] C. Markschies, 'Montanismus' in *Religion in Geschichte und Gegenwart 4*, Tübingen: Mohr Siebeck, vol.5, pp. 1471-2.

Catholic Apostolic Church.[10] An outbreak of Pentecostal phenomena ('speaking in tongues' and claimed miracles of healing) in Port Glasgow in 1829 and later (1831) in the Regent Square Church, London of Edward Irving, led to the founding of a church at what was believed to be the instigation of the Holy Spirit. Twelve Apostles were appointed by the Holy Spirit, who would witness the Second Coming of Christ (the last one died in 1901). This church spread widely in Britain and elsewhere, and its Cathedral in Gordon Square, London was and is a fine piece of architecture. The founding of the movement known as the Assemblies of God in 1914 in Hot Springs, Arizona brought together various Pentecostal movements, and the movement has spread to many parts of the world and is particularly strong in parts of Central and South America. In Britain during the 1960s a Charismatic Movement in the Church of England and other mainstream churches created congregations that stressed 'speaking in tongues' and other gifts of the Spirit.

These modern Pentecostal and Charismatic churches can create problems for Christians who are suspicious of too much emotionalism in religion. The churches often make exaggerated claims about their status as exhibiting true and vibrant Christianity. They can disturb more down-to-earth believers by asserting that only those who 'speak with tongues' are true Christians, or that it is necessary for 'full' Christian belonging to have been 'baptised in the Holy Spirit'. Needless to say, all these movements stress the power aspects of the Holy Spirit; and it has to be conceded that they exist because the main-stream churches have failed

---

[10] C. G. Flegg, *'Gathered Under Apostles' A Study of the Catholic Apostolic Church*, Oxford: Clarendon Press, 1992.

to engage with the doctrine of the Holy Spirit in a way that has enabled 'ordinary believers' to see the church or their lives as enriched by the dimension of the Holy Spirit.

A further difficulty for 'ordinary believers' is one of terminology. The terms 'Father' and 'Son' as applied to God connect with concepts that are familiar to people from their everyday lives, even if they may be misleading as applied to God. 'Holy Spirit' does not connect with anything in everyday lives. The next chapter will try to see how the Holy Spirit can be understood as part of the Holy Trinity.

CHAPTER 2

The Holy Spirit and the Trinity

The doctrine of the Trinity has sometimes been a matter of embarrassment, if not amusement, in the Church of England. It is not unknown for clergy to enter the pulpit on Trinity Sunday apologising for the fact that they feel obliged to say something about the Trinity – a subject that is manifestly alien to them. Yet it can be argued that the Holy Spirit as a 'person' of the Trinity is ignored precisely because the doctrine of the Trinity is lightly regarded in churches. The result is that a vacuum is created that is filled by churches that emphasise the Holy Spirit as a source of power.

The doctrine of the Trinity as it was formulated in the 4th and 5th centuries is not found in the New Testament, but it is certainly implicit, and it is important to be reminded of passages that have a Trinitarian 'ring' to them. In addition to well-known passages such as that containing the 'grace' –

The grace of our Lord Jesus Christ, and the love of God,
and the fellowship of the Holy Ghost, be with us all ever-
more' (2 Corinthians 13.14)

and the command to baptise 'in the name of the Father and
of the Son and of the Holy Ghost' (Matthew 28.19), there are
other less obvious, but sometimes very important,
'Trinitarian' passages. The opening verses of Romans define
the gospel as 'Good News about his [God's] Son, who in the
sphere of the flesh was born of the family of David, in the
sphere of the Holy Spirit was appointed Son of God in
power after his resurrection from the dead.'[11]

One of the difficulties for many churchgoers is caused by the
word 'person' in regard to the 'persons' of the Trinity.
'Person' for modern readers means a distinctive and unique
centre of individuality. As applied to God it suggests three
Gods. In fact, the word 'person' from the Latin 'persona' was
the Latin translation of the Greek prosopon, meaning 'face',
which referred to the masks worn by actors in the theatre.
There were usually only three or four actors in a Greek play,
each of whom played several parts, each distinguished by
the mask worn.[12] In the present work 'person' will be
understood as a distinctive but dependent aspect of God's being
and working. This will now be explored in further detail.

It is often wrongly assumed that the Old Testament is about
God the Father. In fact, the word 'father' for God is rarely
found in the Old Testament and even where it is used, for
example at Isaiah 63.16[13], it cannot, by definition, be under-

---

[11] Translation of Romans 1.3-4 by C.K. Barrett, *The Epistle to the Romans* (Black's New Testament Commentaries), London: A. & C. Black, 1962, p.15.

[12] H.P. Schütt, 'Person' in *Religion in Geschichte und Gegenwart 4*, Tübingen: Mohr Siebeck. vol. 6, 2003, p.1120.

[13] 'Doubtless thou art our father, though Abraham be ignorant of us...'

stood in a Christian sense. The Christian understanding of Father is only possible because of the Son.[14] The term 'father' implies 'son' (or daughter). A human being can be male, but cannot be a father unless he has fathered or adopted a dependent child. In the case of God, he can be called Father only because he has been revealed by his Son, Jesus Christ. The Father and Son are mutually dependent. The Father would not be the Father were it not for the Son; the Son would not be the Son were it not for the Father. However, in spite of their mutual dependence, they are distinctive. It is not the Father who becomes incarnate, lives a human life, and suffers death and rises again, but the Son. The incarnate Son lives in obedience to the Father and surrenders his life to him (Luke 23.46). It is the Father who raises the Son from the dead (Acts 2.24). Yet without the incarnation, life, death and resurrection of the Son, God would not be known as the Father in the Christian sense of the term. The Father and the Son are *distinct but mutually dependent aspects of God's being and working*. How does the Holy Spirit fit into this scheme?

A question that is sometimes asked about the divinity of Jesus is how Jesus can be God when he is living a human life on earth. Who is running the universe if God is temporarily living a human life on earth? Also, when Jesus prays to God, is he speaking to himself? It was to answer such questions that the doctrine of the Trinity had to be worked out. If there is a third *distinctive but dependent aspect of God's being and working*, there is an answer to the question who was running the universe during the incarnation. The Holy Spirit is the

---

[14] What follows here is indebted to W. Pannenberg, *Systematische Theologie*, Band 1, Göttingen: Vandenhoeck & Ruprecht, 1988, pp. 283-364.

name for God in action in the world. He is Spirit in that God is not material; he is Holy in that sense of 'holy' which means 'belonging properly to God'. He is a 'person' of the Trinity in the sense that he enables God (as revealed in Jesus Christ) to be known in a personal way to human beings. This does not exhaust his work, as will be considered in other sections of this book; but it is an essential part of his work. The writers of the New Testament had a vivid awareness that God was at work among them; that where people responded in faith to the preaching of the gospel, this was the work of the Holy Spirit. This work was 'Trinitarian' in that the gospel was the good news of what God had done in Jesus Christ. Those who came to faith did so as the Holy Spirit made real to them the love of God as made known in Jesus Christ.

One of the reasons why many churches today lack a sense of God at work among them, and lack a sense that they are living in a new age brought about by the ministry of Jesus, is because the work of the Holy Spirit has been thought to operate only at special times or in extraordinary happenings. On the one hand, the idea of the Holy Spirit as a gift administered by the action of a bishop led to the view that only when a bishop was confirming or ordaining was the Holy Spirit in any way active. On the other hand, emphasis on 'gifts of the Spirit' such as 'speaking in tongues' led to the view that unless something spectacular was happening the Holy Spirit was not present and active.

A later chapter will examine Paul's teaching on the Holy Spirit. For the moment, however, an important passage from 1 Corinthians 12 will be discussed. There were evidently members of the church at Corinth who believed, as do many pentecostal and charismatic Christians today, that 'speaking in tongues' was an infallible guide to the activity of the Holy Spirit in the church. Paul did not disagree, and neither is it the purpose of this book to disagree. However, Paul devoted three chapters of 1 Corinthians to putting the matter into perspective. In the process he provided valuable guidance for Christians of subsequent ages. Here is the passage (1 Corinthians 12.4-11).

> Now there are diversities of gifts, but the same Spirit; and there are differences of administrations, but the same Lord; And there are diversities of operations, but it is the same God which worketh all in all. But the manifestation of the Spirit is given to every man to profit withal. For to one is given by the Spirit the word of wisdom; to another the word of knowledge by the same Spirit; To another faith by the same Spirit; to another the gifts of healing by the same Spirit; To another the working of miracles; to another prophecy; to another discerning of spirits; to another divers kinds of tongues; to another the interpretation of tongues. But all these worketh that one and the selfsame Spirit, dividing to every man severally as he will.

The first thing to note here is the Trinitarian formula: the same Spirit, the same Lord (i.e. Christ), the same God.[15] The next point is that although the list refers to phenomena such as 'speaking in tongues' which would be spectacular, these come at the end, and are preceded by operations that are not necessarily spectacular: the utterance of wisdom, the utterance of knowledge, the possession of an unusually intense measure of faith[16], the gift of healing (which ought not to exclude healing by medical knowledge). Paul, even if this is

---

[15] C.K.Barrett, *The First Epistle to the Corinthians* (Black's New Testament Commentaries), London: A. & C. Black, 1968, p.284.

[16] J. Héring, *La première épitre de Saint Paul aux Corinthiens* (Commentaire du Nouveau Testament), Neuchatel: Delachaux & Niestlé, 1959 (2nd ed.), p .109.

not his main intention, can be said to be describing *ordinary* things taking place in the church, such as teaching, advising, supporting, comforting, and saying that even if these operations are ordinary and not spectacular, they are still the work of the Holy Spirit. If Christians today can think of the church as the place where things are done for the sake of Jesus Christ by the working of the Holy Spirit (he also works outside the church, of course), a big step will have been taken towards rediscovering the presence and thus the power of the Spirit in the church.

If the attempt in this chapter to understand the Holy Spirit as a 'person' in the Trinity has been at all successful, there remains the task of relating this to the idea of the Holy Spirit as a gift, as power, and as indwelling believers. The first step is comparatively easy. If the Holy Spirit is a 'gift' this depends entirely and utterly upon the initiative and free action of God. To put it in other words, God gives himself as Spirit freely and unexpectedly. The idea that God's self-giving can be confined to and channelled via any human agency such as bishops or even the first apostles, must be rejected. If the evidence of Acts is examined closely it is clear that although the writer in some cases connects the giving of the Spirit with the laying on of hands, this is not an invariable pattern.[17] What, then, are we to make of the passages that do link the gift of the Spirit with the laying on of hands? One possible solution is to interpret passages such as Acts 8.14-17 as describing how the spread of the gospel to non-Jews was authorised by the Jerusalem apostles and authenticated by the outward signs that the Spirit had been 'received'. As Barrett comments, 'The mission to Samaria (which is what

---

[17] Barrett, *Acts* vol.1, p.412.

the passage is about) is part of the movement whose links with Jesus are affirmed by the apostles whom he chose. It is part of a wider mission inspired by the Spirit, who is Lord over the process'.[18] The passage in Acts 19.1-7 can be interpreted in a similar manner. Here, Paul comes across around twelve disciples in Ephesus who had only received John the Baptist's baptism, and knew nothing of the Holy Spirit. He explains how John looked forward to the coming of Jesus. After they are baptised into the name of the Lord Jesus, Paul lays hands upon them and they 'receive' the Holy Spirit. This may be seen as an indication of how disciples of John the Baptist were to be received into the church, with the visible sign of the Spirit's 'descent' (i.e. 'speaking in tongues') authenticating the admission process.[19] An attempt still needs to be made to link the laying on of hands with the 'giving' of the Spirit.

To receive the Spirit was to become aware in a new way of the nature of God and his love for the world in the ministry and death of Jesus. It meant being able to understand what Paul meant when he wrote of 'the Son of God who loved me and gave himself for me' (Galatians 2.20). This 'becoming aware' was an event in the life of individuals, an event initiated by the Holy Spirit (i.e. God in action) and bringing about a permanent change in the outlooks of those affected, a permanent change that could be called the gift of the Spirit, or the 'indwelling' of the Spirit. The laying on of hands could not have been simply a mechanism for imparting this new awareness. It may, however, have been the culmination of a number of actions including preaching, teaching, prayer,

---

[18] Barrett, *Acts* , vol.1, p.411.

[19] See also Barrett, *Acts* vol 2, p.898.

and physical contact designed to reinforce the spoken words. The outcome was *personal*. To have 'received' the Holy Spirit was not to have been injected with some life-enhancing potency, but to have become aware of the love of God in a way that affected the human emotions and intellect, in the way that falling in love with another person affects human emotions and the intellect. For some, the impact upon the emotions may have been sufficient to release in them the ecstatic language called 'speaking in tongues' but this was not an inevitable or universal outcome of 'receiving' the Spirit. As Paul says to the Corinthians, 'do all speak with tongues?' with the implied answer being 'no'! (1 Corinthians 12.30)

It is important in Christian theology and practice to stress the primacy of the Holy Spirit as a *person* over the Holy Spirit as *power* or *influence*. These two ways of viewing the Holy Spirit have quite different implications and practical outcomes. If attention is concentrated upon power and influence, results will be looked for as evidence of the presence and working of the power. The absence of 'results' will lead to the conclusion that there is no power, and thus no Holy Spirit. The whole focus of attention will be upon *human* achievements, however much those are obscured by pious language about the Holy Spirit. There is the danger that there will be a craving for 'results', results of a spectacular nature. Such cravings can in turn become addictive, producing the desire for ever more spectacular evidences of the presence of the Spirit. Further, these evidences will be used to enhance the standing of those humans who are producing or witnessing the spectacular signs and wonders, however much the glory may be assigned to God. At its worst, and the case has been admittedly and deliberately overstated, the outcome can be an exercise in extreme selfishness and self-centredness, magnified and obscured by the religious language and practice that surrounds it.

The opposite approach, which begins from the Holy Spirit as a 'person' (*a distinctive but dependent aspect of God's being and working*) who makes us aware that God in Jesus Christ loves us and is for us, should never in principle lead to the self-preoccupation that can arise when the Holy Spirit is viewed as a power. The whole point of the witness of the Holy Spirit to what God has done for us in Christ is that this work is undeserved and in some ways incredible. 'For scarcely for a righteous man will one die' exclaims Paul at Romans 5.7-8, 'but God commendeth his love toward us, in that, while we were yet sinners, Christ died for us'. Paul, indeed, is the outstanding example of the believer whose personal experiences of the Holy Spirit led to humility, not pride. Time and again, especially in 2 Corinthians, a letter full of references to the Holy Spirit, Paul checks himself when tempted to boast of his achievements. If he is to boast, it must be of his weaknesses because only then can God use him effectively (2 Corinthians 12.9-10, cp. Galatians 6.14).

Another important outcome of concentration upon the Spirit as a 'person' working among believers (and not only believers) is that it is possible to begin to see the Spirit working in many 'ordinary' things, and thus to develop a sense that Christians are living in the dimension of the Spirit, while at the same time living in an as-yet unredeemed world. The passage from 1 Corinthians 12 has been noted above, with its mention of non-spectacular operations that are the work of the Spirit. Struggling churches and believers can be encouraged to discover the Spirit at work among them. If one of the tasks of the Holy Spirit is to bear witness to the ministry of Jesus, he is witnessing to something that was humanly speaking a failure. The ministry of Jesus ended in crucifixion, and his closest followers deserted him. If the Holy Spirit is thought of only as power, there is no room for failure, and struggling congregations are signs of his absence. If the Holy Spirit is present in struggling churches that are seeking to bear witness to Jesus, members can be encouraged in their work. They are as much places where the Spirit is at work as are successful charismatic churches. This realisation could have transforming effects.

This chapter has tried to stress the importance of seeing the Holy Spirit as a 'person' of the Trinity, and has tried to relate that to experiences of the Spirit as power or influence. The next chapter will explore other aspects of the presence and working of the Holy Spirit in the world.

CHAPTER 3

The Holy Spirit and the World

The subject of how the Holy Spirit is active in the world is one that sharply divides theologians. In a much-praised book on the Holy Spirit[20], J. V. Taylor divided theologians between those who disconnected God and nature, and those who wished to see the activity of God in nature.[21] In Taylor's view the Holy Spirit, thought of as the Go-Between God, was a way of bridging the gap between the material and spiritual worlds. In a memorable phrase Taylor claimed that Paul's vision of the world of nature in travail waiting for the adoption of the sons of God (Romans 8.18-23) meant that we are to find God 'always on the inside of creation'.[22] This further meant that God was not to be found in the gaps but in the processes of nature; not in special interventions, but in continuous processes. Taylor went on to consider the work of scientists who spoke of 'awarenesses' of particles of matter, and concluded

---

[20] J. V. Taylor, *The Go-Between God. The Holy Spirit and the Christian Mission*, London: SCM Press, 1972.

[21] Taylor, *Go-Between God*, pp. 42-3.

[22] Taylor, *Go-Between God*, pp. 27-8.

As a believer in the Creator Spirit I would say that deep within the fabric of the universe, therefore, the Spirit is present as the Go-Between who confronts each isolated spontaneous particle with the beckoning reality of the larger whole and so compels it to relate to others in a particular way; and that it is he who at every stage lures the inner organisms forward by giving an inner awareness and recognition of the unattained.[23]

In what follows, I shall disagree with Taylor, while wanting to endorse his statement that we are to find God 'always on the inside of creation'. His position raises philosophical and theological questions.

Recent scientific and philosophical writers have discussed whether there is what is called 'self-organisation' in nature. By this is meant the possibility that within processes of nature there are forces at work that guide inter-related causes to achieve certain 'ends'.[24] The difficulty with this, as Karen Gloy points out[25] is that it involves arguing in a circle, and depends on the fallacy of *petitio principii*, i.e. assuming in the premise what is asserted in the conclusion. The notion of 'self-organisation' is brought by the observer to the phenomena that are observed, and can in no verifiable way be simply read out of the natural processes. The same charge can be brought against the writers on whom Taylor depends. There is simply no way of knowing whether there is 'awareness' in primary particles of matter, and the belief that there might be involves reading into scientific observation the

[23] Taylor, *Go-Between God*, p. 31.

[24] See the essay by K. Gloy, 'Schellings Naturphilosophie. Grundzüge und Kritik' in R. Hiltscher, S. Klinger, (eds.), *Friedrich Wilhelm Joseph Schelling* (Neue Wege der Forschung), Darmstadt: Wissenschaftliche Buchgesellschaft, 2012, p.99, where reference is made to J. Monod, *Zufall und Notwendigkeit, Philosphische Fragen der modernen Biologie*, Munich, 1971.

[25] Gloy, 'Schellings Naturphilosophie', p. 99.

human notion of 'awareness'. A further problem of the kind of approach favoured by Taylor is that it has to confront the problem of natural evil. If the Holy Spirit is in some way involved in natural processes, is he responsible for those things that are dangerous to human life? The view taken in this book is that there is no relationship between philosophical theories of nature and exact scientific observation and experimentation[26] and that the same should apply to theological speculation.

This does not mean that we have to accept the view, so distasteful to Taylor, that 'God is so absolutely distinct from his creation that nothing can be known about him by inference from the facts of the world'.[27] It does mean that it is necessary to think carefully about how the Holy Spirit relates to nature, and what can be said about this. There is an interesting note in O.C. Quick's *Catholic and Protestant Elements in Christianity* about the *compresence* of God that deserves to be quoted in full.

> [God] is universally *compresent*. By that we mean that all things are in direct relation to God, and are what they are because of that relation, though, of course, it does not follow that God is to be identified with all things. Thus evil is evil, and error is error, because they are in direct relation to God's omnipresent goodness and truth, though the direct relation is here one of opposition. God therefore is present in every conceivable situation, and all response of any organism to any environment must be directly a response to God.[28]

---

[26] Gloy, 'Schellings Naturphilosophie', p. 101.

[27] Taylor: *Go-Between God*, p. 42

[28] O. C. Quick, *Catholic and Protestant Elements in Christianity*, London: Longmans, Green and Co., 1924, p.61.

I am not sure in this statement what the word 'direct' adds to the word 'relation', and I would be happier without it. Also, I do not know whether I would want to say that the response of *any* organism must be 'directly' a response to God. What I like about the statement is that it affirms a relationship between God and the world without implying an identity between them. God's *compresence* shows evil and error to be what they are without making God responsible for them. If, for God, we say the Holy Spirit (God in action) then we have a theological statement that relates the Spirit to the world without claiming to know how this works in detail, and we do not intrude onto the territory of the natural sciences. A further step is suggested by the two subtle essays of A. Clutton-Brock in the symposium *The Spirit*.[29]

Clutton-Brock's theme in the first essay can be summed up as follows. It is the role of the Spirit to make us aware of beauty in nature and art in such a way that we are touched and moved by it *personally*. He criticises the 'scientific' view that it alone can explain the 'impersonal world of things, functions, and processes' insisting that such explanation is 'not the whole of reality as we experience it'. He points out that in music 'art escapes from all facts that can be seen or stated in words or paint' while at the same time touching and moving us personally.[30]

In the second essay, Clutton-Brock asks what is happening when we perceive beauty and truth in nature and art. His answer is that we are perceiving not objects, but what he

---

[29] A. Clutton-Brock, 'Spiritual Experience' and 'Spirit and Matter' in B. H. Streeter (ed.), *The Spirit, God and his relation to man considered from the standpoint of Philosophy, Psychology and Art*, London: Macmillan, 1919, pp. 279-309, 312-346.

[30] Clutton-Brock, 'Spiritual Experience', pp. 284-5.

calls universal relations, and he relates this perception to what he calls the human spirit. To be aware of these universal relations has another important side. The most important thing about beauty is that it is not *useful*.[31] To see objects as beautiful is to see them in a new way: not as objects, but as indicators of something else that can be of no direct use to us but which can make us aware of a realm of values that we do not wish to master (we would destroy them if we did), but which we desire to master us. This in turn changes our relation to nature as a whole. In opposition to technical reason, which sees nature as an object to be used for the benefit of the human race – and there is nothing wrong in this in principle – nature becomes a realm of spiritual experience in which we encounter awe, wonder and beauty. What is, in fact, being encountered is the Spirit of God, not as something *in* nature, but someone that enables us to encounter nature in a personal way.

An approach along these lines enables us to achieve Taylor's goal – to affirm that God is on the inside of his creation - without questionable uses of scientific thought, or the dangers of panentheism (seeing God in everything). It enables us to appreciate the Holy Spirit as the one who speaks to us through our contemplation of the world of nature, and through the beauty that is expressed in the arts and music. It enables us to see the world in a spiritual way, one that we can then relate to the Holy Spirit as a person of the Trinity, who reveals to us God in Jesus Christ.

---

[31] Clutton-Brock, 'Spirit and Matter', pp.320-1.

This approach is actually biblical. The Bible will be discussed in detail in later chapters. For the moment attention will be drawn to several texts. In Psalm 8.3-4 the psalmist declares

> For I will comsider thy heavens,
> even the work of thy fingers;
> the moon and the stars which thou hast ordained.
> What is man, that thou art mindful of him:
> And the son of man, that thou visitest him?

The psalmist sees the heavens and the moon and stars not merely as objects. They beget in him an experience of awe and wonder. These experiences are not *useful* to him in any practical way. They point beyond the objects themselves to a transcendent reality above the comprehension of the psalmist, yet one in which he can utter words of prayer and praise. There can be no doubt that the Spirit of God is here at work.

In the New Testament Jesus asks his hearers to consider the birds of the air and the lilies of the field (Matthew 6.25-33). Not even Solomon in all his glory was arrayed like one of the lilies, even though its life-span is so short. The conclusion that Jesus asks his hearers to draw seems odd at first sight: do not be anxious about what to eat, or drink, or wear. This oddness is easier to understand if we approach the passage as follows. The birds and the lilies can become a source for our experience of awe and wonder. We see beyond the objects themselves to intimations of eternal values. Although eating, drinking and clothing are not unimportant, they do not belong immediately to the world of the spirit to which awe and wonder point. It is no accident that the passage ends with the plea to seek first God's kingdom and his righteousness. God's kingdom is the sum-total of the eternal values of truth, beauty and harmony, not simply in a heavenly realm beyond human existence, but a realm brought near to human experience by the activity of God's Spirit.

The Holy Spirit and history

The first part of this chapter has considered the relation of the Holy Spirit to nature; the second part will consider his relation to history. On the face of it, this is an easier topic than that of the Spirit's relation to nature. History is not about non-human life and processes but about human events. History is shaped by human decisions, and these can be influenced by the Spirit of God. Further, Christian theology has deep roots going back to biblical times, which enables it to assert that human events are things in which God is involved and in which he reveals himself. 'It was not you who sent me here, but God' says Joseph to his brothers when he reveals his identity to them in the Egypt into which they had sold him (Genesis 45.8). This passage has been used by 19th and 20th century biblical scholars as evidence of a 'modern' view of history, as a process led by God.[32] Perhaps it is not surprising that the nineteenth century, buoyed by the Idea of progress, should find it easy to view history as a process guided by God (i.e. the Spirit of God).[33] That twentieth-century biblical scholars should have found this plausible, given the horrors of world wars and genocides that occurred in the twentieth century, is harder to understand.

The term 'history' is of course problematic, as are the ways in which it can be written. Should 'history' be an account of

---

[32] See J.W.Rogerson, 'Can a Doctrine of Providence be based on the Old Testament?' in L. Eslinger, G. Taylor (eds.) *Ascribe to the Lord, Biblical and other studies in memory of Peter C. Craigie*, Sheffield: Sheffield Academic Press, 1988, pp. 529-43.

[33] See J. Rogerson, *Old Testament Criticism in the Nineteenth Century. England and Germany*, London: SPCK, 1984, pp.104-112, 121-129.

the doings of influential men and women, or should it analyse the economic and social factors that 'drive' the course of history? Elsewhere, I have described and defended my acceptance of the narrative view of history: that it is something that we narrate, dependent on our possession of artifacts from the past, and the special interests that we bring to the narration.[34] When allowances have been made for these difficulties and uncertainties the following points can be made. First, while the impact of individuals upon events must always depend upon times and circumstances, there is no doubt that individuals can decisively affect the course of events. Martin Luther's reforms were no doubt greatly helped by the invention of printing and revival of the study of Greek and Hebrew. However, there can be no doubt that Luther's intense personal religious experience and insights played a major part in the movement which he initiated. It would be reasonable to claim that God's Spirit, working through Luther, brought about the Reformation. The work of the Holy Spirit can thus be discerned in his influence upon men and women who have shaped human affairs.

Secondly, it must also be acknowledged that there have been leaders whose actions have affected human affairs disastrously. Adolf Hitler's rise to power was made possible by the state of Europe following the First World War. Presumably, no one would want to claim that Hitler was guided by the Holy Spirit. This means, thirdly, that if we want to argue that God's Spirit is in some way active in 'history', this must be done in a way that disassociates him from direct responsibility for the catastrophes of human history. Quick's idea

---

[34] J. W. Rogerson, *A Theology of the Old Testament. Cultural Memory, communication and being human*, London: SPCK, 2009, pp. 13-41.

of God's *compresence* is helpful here.[35] We may say that the presence of the Holy Spirit in human affairs (however we envisage that presence) shows such affairs to be good or evil in relation to the Spirit's own goodness. We can also say that where good comes out of evil, this is thanks to the work of the Holy Spirit.

A later chapter will discuss the work of the Holy Spirit as seen in the Old Testament and its historical books. For the moment, mention can be made of Georg Fohrer's view that Old Testament narratives are *decision history* in which the choices made by Israelite rulers and people highlight moral alternatives.[36] The Spirit can be seen at work there by confronting people with moral choices. In this way we can attune ourselves to seeing that God is on the *inside* of his creation, in connection with historical events, while fully recognising the many features of human activity that are contrary to God's will.

The Holy Spirit and the individual

Christians often pray, and sing hymns, in which they ask to be guided by the Holy Spirit. Fortunately, there is usually no way in which it is possible to know whether, and if so, how, such wishes have been answered. I write 'fortunately', because it is easy for us to use God as a means of obtaining what we desire, and to pray hoping that the Holy Spirit will somehow endorse what *we* have decided is best for us. It is usually only from the point of view of hindsight that we can get some inkling that we have been guided by the Holy

---

[35] See above, p.21.

[36] G. Fohrer, *Geschichte der israelitischen Religion*, Berlin: de Gruyter, 1969, pp. 278-9; English Translation. *History of Israelite Religion*, London: SPCK, 1973, pp. 275-6.

Spirit. Such hindsight is not to be despised, however, as long as it becomes a basis for humility and not boasting. It is a humbling thought that the Holy Spirit (the active presence of the Creator God) should be involved in the details of lives of beings who are but the tiniest specks in space and time. Yet this is what the New Testament affirms: that the Spirit bears witness with our spirit that we are the children of God, heirs of God and fellow-heirs with Christ (Romans 8.16-17). The God who declares his love for us in Christ and makes us his children is the one who is concerned for the details of our lives. He is *compresent*, not violating our freedom or overruling our decisions, but seeking to make all things work together for our good (Romans 8.28). This is a promise not just to those who have or exercise 'gifts of the Spirit' but to all believers. It is important for all believers that they should know what has been promised and should live in the faith and hope that God's Spirit is *compresent* in their lives.

CHAPTER 4

Jesus and the Holy Spirit

In his study *The Holy Spirit and the Gospel Tradition*, C. K. Barrett drew attention to a curious paradox.[37] The early church, as portrayed in the Acts of the Apostles and the Pauline letters, was convinced that it was empowered and guided by the Holy Spirit; that it owed its existence not only to the ministry of Jesus, but to the 'outpouring' of the Holy Spirit after the death and resurrection of Jesus. However, in the first three Gospels there are very few references to the

---

[37] C. K. Barrett, *The Holy Spirit and the Gospel Tradition*, London: SPCK, 1966 (new edition), pp. 1-3.

Holy Spirit, and Jesus himself appears to have said almost nothing about the subject. The task of Barrett's book is to account for this paradox, and the present chapter is deeply indebted to it; but it will also seek to contribute some original ideas and to draw practical conclusions for today's church. A preliminary observation is that the lack of reference to the Holy Spirit in the first three Gospels, Gospels written for churches that believed themselves to be the location of the Spirit's work, indicates the honest way in which the Gospel tradition tried to represent the work and words of Jesus. They did not try to read back into his life, words or evidence about the Holy Spirit that were not there in his ministry.

The birth of Jesus

The part played by the Holy Spirit in the birth of Jesus is described explicitly in Luke's Gospel and implicitly in Matthew's. In Luke 1.26-38 Mary is visited by the angel Gabriel and told that she will have a son. To Mary's rejoinder that she has no husband, the angel replies that 'The Holy Ghost shall come upon thee, and the power of the Highest shall overshadow thee' (Luke 1.35). In Matthew an angel appears to Joseph in a dream and assures him that 'that which is conceived in her (Mary) is of the Holy Ghost' (Matthew 1.20).

The reading of the story of the Annunciation (i.e. Luke 1.26 - 38) is so familiar to churchgoers and others as part of the 'Christmas story' that it is not easy to view it critically. Some may have no difficulty in taking the story literally. Others will see it as a type of story that uses figures drawn from how people imagine the supernatural world to be, in order to describe unusual features of the world of time and space.

The issue is not whether there are such things as angels that appear to people and converse with them. The issue is whether we believe that the Creator God works on the inside of his creation. In the case of Jesus it should be his ministry, death and resurrection that move people to believe that 'God was in Christ' (2 Corinthians 5.19), not stories about his birth, and here it must be regretted that the large numbers of people who come to attend carol services at Christmas time are not in evidence on Good Friday and Easter Day. The view taken here is that however Jesus was conceived, and whatever part the Holy Spirit took in this process, the stories in Luke and Matthew state that the life of Jesus was uniquely the action of God. The stories tell us nothing about the mechanics of the birth of Jesus or the action of the Holy Spirit in his conception.

The commentators devote much space to trying to discover parallels in Jewish and Greek tradition to the idea of the Holy Spirit being involved in the birth of a divine being, largely without success.[38] Barrett concludes that the idea has its roots in the interpretation of the Old Testament among Hellenistic Jews (i.e. Jews living in the Greek-speaking parts of the Roman Empire). The presence of the Spirit of God at creation (Genesis 1.2) is paralleled by the presence of the Holy Spirit at the very beginning of the new creation that God begins with the birth of Jesus. [39]

The baptism of Jesus
The first three Gospels record that Jesus was baptised by John the Baptist, but they differ over the precise words

---

[38] See the extensive discussion in Barrett, *The Holy Spirit*, pp.6-24.

[39] Barrett, *The Holy Spirit*, pp. 23-4.

spoken by the voice from heaven. More importantly, whereas Mark 1.9-10 portrays the outcome of the baptism in terms of what Jesus alone experiences (similarly Matthew 3.16-17), Luke 3.21-2 suggests that the descent of the Holy Spirit and the voice from heaven were phenomena that could have been observed by others present. All three Gospels are agreed that the descent of the Holy Spirit and the speaking of the voice from heaven happened *after*, not during the baptism. This is made most explicit by Luke: 'that Jesus also being baptized, and praying, the heaven was opened...' (Luke 3.21). The point of this separation between the baptism and the opening of heaven may have been to make it clear that John the Baptist's baptism did not 'convey' the Holy Spirit.[40]

The main issue for a modern reader is whether the Markan account (presumably the earliest, and the source for Matthew and Luke) records an inner experience of Jesus which he then at some stage described to the disciples, or whether it is an interpretation by the Gospel tradition of the fact that Jesus had been baptised by John. It must be allowed that being baptised was for Jesus a profound experience of being commissioned and empowered by God. The view taken here, however, is that the narrative is an interpretation by the Gospel tradition. There are two reasons for this. First, as has already been pointed out, the narrative is at pains to stress that the heavens opened *after* not during the baptism. If this is to dissociate John's baptism from the 'descent' of the Holy Spirit, there is already an interpretative element in the narrative. Secondly, and this point will feature importantly

---

[40] J. Gnilka, *Das Evangelium nach Markus* (Evangelisch-Katholischer Kommentar zum Neuen Testament) II/1, Zürich: Benzinger Verlag, 1998 (5th ed), pp. 51-2.

in the present chapter, Jesus (as presented in the first three Gospels) was reluctant to claim publicly that he was the Messiah or Son of God. This reluctance was to avoid the misunderstanding that inevitably arose in connection with such designations.[41] The Gospel tradition interpreted the baptism of Jesus to emphasise things that the church believed about Jesus - that he was the chosen servant and Son of God and that he was empowered in his mission by the Spirit of God. These convictions may well have been confirmed for Jesus at, and because of, his baptism. Whether they took the form that is described in the Gospel accounts is another matter.

Barrett devotes a whole chapter to investigating the possible sources for the imagery and language of the account of the baptism, noting Old Testament statements about the Spirit of God empowering prophets and other chosen servants. The Jewish background to the voice from heaven is also investigated – the so-called *bat qol*, literally, 'daughter of a voice' – a kind of echo of the divine voice, mentioned in Jewish sources. There is a parallel with Genesis 1.2 where the Spirit of God hovers over the primal waters out of which the world is ordered. The bird-like associations of the word 'hovered' (Hebrew *merahephet*) connect with the image of the dove.[42]

What this amounts to is that we must be very cautious in making claims about the Holy Spirit on the basis of the narrative of the baptism of Jesus. Claims that Jesus 'received'

[41] This point is particularly emphasised by Barrett, *The Holy Spirit*, pp. 160-162.

[42] Barrett, *The Holy Spirit*, esp. pp.35-45. The reason for the dove symbolism has not been satisfactorily explained, unless L. E. Keck ('The Spirit and the Dove', *New Testament Studies* 17 (1970/71), pp. 41-67) is correct, that the Gospel narrative is saying that the Holy Spirit was descending 'dove-like' rather than in the form of a dove.

or was 'baptised in' the Holy Spirit at his baptism must be treated with caution. They are symptoms of the desire to link the Holy Spirit only with spectacular happenings. They invite the question 'was Jesus *not* guided or taught by the Holy Spirit prior to his baptism?'

The temptations of Jesus

The first three Gospels are agreed that the baptism of Jesus was followed by the temptations in the wilderness. Mark covers the incident in two verses (Mark 1.12-13); Matthew (4.1-11) and Luke (4.1-13) have accounts that are almost identical except for the order of the temptations. All three Gospels agree that it was the Holy Spirit that moved Jesus to spend time in the wilderness. It is possible to see a link between the baptism and the temptations in the following way. If, as a result of the baptism, Jesus was in some new way empowered or assured by the presence of the Holy Spirit, the outcome was not an immediate display of spectacular power by Jesus, but his withdrawal from public life into a solitude in which he rejected the tempter's suggestions that he should use his power to demonstrate his role as the Son of God.

Barrett[43] investigates the possible background to the temptations story with his usual thoroughness and concludes that each temptation is 'messianic' in that it can be connected with the fulfilment of an expectation that was entertained about what the Messiah would do when he was revealed.[44] However, what the tempter explicitly questions is not whether Jesus is the Messiah, but whether he is the Son of God

[43] Barrett, *The Holy Spirit*, pp.46-53.

[44] See especially Barrett, *The Holy Spirit*, pp.51-2: the Messiah would give manna to the people of God or would stand on the roof of the Temple.

(Matthew 4.3,6). Fitzmyer[45] is surely correct to see in the tempter's words a reference back to the baptism, where the voice from heaven declared 'thou art my Son' (Mark 1.11; cp. Luke 3.22 'thou art my beloved Son'; Matthew 3.17 'this is my beloved Son'). The purpose of the narrative, however it relates to what may have been the personal experience of Jesus at the time, is to confirm what the heavenly voice stated: that Jesus is the Son of God, even if the response of Jesus to the suggestions of the tempter redefines what is meant by 'Son of God' in unexpected ways.

If this line of argument is correct, it has implications for how the Holy Spirit is understood in the narrative. The Holy Spirit is responsible for a set of incidents (the temptations) that define in an unexpected way what it means for Jesus to be the Son of God. His mission is to be accomplished without recourse to spectacular demonstrations of power. To be guided by the Holy Spirit means, for Jesus, to work in hidden and unspectacular ways. How does this claim make sense of the miracles and exorcisms performed by Jesus? Surely, these are spectacular demonstrations of the work of the Holy Spirit in his ministry.

The exorcisms and miracles

In Mark there are four narratives that describe exorcisms performed by Jesus (Mark 1.23-27, 5.1-20, 7.24-30, 9.14-29) although summary passages such as Mark 1.32-34 and 3.11-12 imply that these four explicit accounts do not cover all the occasions on which Jesus performed exorcisms. Of the narratives in Mark, Matthew omits the exorcism at Capernaum

---

[45] J.A.Fitzmyer, *The Gospel according to Luke I-IX*, (The Anchor Bible), New Haven: Yale University Press, 1970, p. 515.

(Mark 1.23-27) and Luke omits the exorcism of the daughter of the Syro-Phoenician woman (Mark 7.24-30), while in Matthew the account of the exorcism of the Gadarene demoniac (Mark 5.1-20) is considerably abbreviated. There is one account of an exorcism common to Matthew (12.22-24) and Luke (11.14-16) not found in Mark, but it gives few details. This is the introduction in Matthew and Luke to the Beelzebul Controversy, in which Jesus is accused of casting out dem-ons by Beelzebul (Matthew 12.25-37, Luke 11.17-23; cp. Mark 3.23-30). Only Matthew records (briefly) the healing of a dumb demoniac (Matthew 9.32-34), and only Luke (Luke 13.10-17) has the account of the healing of a woman 'with a spirit of infirmity' who is described by Jesus as having been bound by Satan. Among the list of women who (according to Luke 8.1-3) formed part of the entourage of Jesus on his preaching journeys was Mary Magdalene 'out of whom went seven devils'. To those narratives should be added the information that Jesus gave to the twelve disciples 'power against unclean spirits, to cast them out' (Matthew 10.1; cp. Mark 6.7, Luke 9.1).

It is well known that people in the ancient world believed in the existence of demons, that demons could and did 'possess' people and that there were exorcists who could 'expel' demons. Barrett cites parallels from classical and Jewish sources, to which can be added the section on Rabbinic Judaism in Urbach.[46] Barrett concludes that, as an exorcist, Jesus, according to the Gospels, was *'in no way significant...*

---

[46] Barrett, *The Holy Spirit*, pp.53-57; E.E. Urbach, *Hazal-Pirqe emunoth vedeot*, Jerusalem: Magnes Press, 1971, pp. 94-100 (Hebrew); English Translation. *The Sages : Their Concepts and Beliefs*, Jerusalem: Magnes Press, 1975, pp. 112-119.

his power to cast out demons did not differentiate him from other men'.[47]

One of the striking things about the exorcism narratives in the first three Gospels is their complete lack of reference to the Holy Spirit. The only possible exception is in Matthew 12.28, in the Beelzebul Controversy. Jesus says 'if I cast out devils by the Spirit of God, then the Kingdom of God is come unto you'. However, the parallel passage in Luke 11.20 has 'finger of God'. Given that Luke emphasises the Holy Spirit more than the other Gospels[48] it is widely held that Luke's version of the saying, without the Holy Spirit, is more likely to represent what Jesus actually said.[49] In fact, the purpose of the exorcism narrative is not to present Jesus as a 'charismatic' person, but to show two things: that he is the Son of God, and that in this ministry, the Kingdom of God is present.

In Mark 1.24 and 5.7 the demons possessing the people whom Jesus meets recognise who Jesus is. You are the 'Holy One of God' says one (Mark 1.24) while the demon possessing the Gerasene demoniac asks 'what have I to do with thee, Jesus, thou Son of the most high God?' (Mark 5.7). In the Beelzebul Controversy (Matthew 12.24-29, Luke 11.14 - 23) the issue is whether Jesus casts out demons because he is somehow part of Satan's kingdom, or whether his exorcisms are a manifestation of the presence of God's kingdom in his ministry. The second alternative is supported by the argu-

---

[47] Barrett, *The Holy Spirit*, p.68, italics those of Barrett.

[48] See Fitzmyer, *Luke I-IX*, p. 227.

[49] Barrett, *The Holy Spirit*, pp.62-3; U.Luz, *Das Evangelium nach Matthäus* (Evangelisch-Katholischer Kommentar zum Neuen Testament) 1/ 2 3, Zürich: Benzinger Verlag; Neukirchen-Vluyn: Neukirchener Verlag, 1996 (2nd ed.), p.255.

ment that if Jesus is part of Satan's realm, then that realm is in a state of anarchy because Satan is casting out Satan (Matthew 12.26). It is *not* the purpose of the exorcism stories in the first three Gospels to show that Jesus is a 'charismatic' person.

The same can be said about the authority that Jesus gives to the disciples to cast out demons (Matthew 10.1, Luke 9.1; cp. Mark 6.7). In no case is this authority or power attributed to the Holy Spirit. From other passages we can gather that it was the use of the *name* of Jesus that was effective in casting out demons (Matthew 7.22, Mark 9.38, Luke 10.17).[50] If this is correct, there is here an implicit recognition of the divinity of Jesus. His *name* is effective because of who he is.

The authority given by Jesus to his disciples during his lifetime raises two questions. First, if the disciples successfully used his *name* (see Luke 10.17) did they recognise his divinity at the time, and if so, why did they react so badly during and after the Passion of Jesus? Second, were the exorcisms performed by the disciples during the ministry of Jesus made possible by the Holy Spirit? If they were, then the disciples were empowered by the Spirit *before* the day of Pentecost. If their exorcisms were not the work of the Holy Spirit, then it is wrong to link the casting out of demons with the presence of the Holy Spirit. This second question is rhetorical. The answer to the first question is that if the disciples did believe in the divinity of Jesus during his ministry, this belief was shattered when Jesus allowed himself to be arrested, imprisoned and crucified.

---

[50] See Barrett, *The Holy Spirit*, pp. 66 and 127-30.

The sin against the Holy Spirit

A very difficult saying of Jesus on this subject is recorded in all three of the first Gospels.

Matthew 12.31-2	Mark 3.28-9	Luke 12.10
Wherefore I say unto you, All manner of sin and blasphemy shall be forgiven unto men; but the blasphemy against the Holy Ghost shall not be forgiven unto men. And whosoever speaketh a word against the Son of Man, it shall be forgiven him: but whosoever speaketh against the Holy Ghost, it shall not be forgiven him, neither in this world, neither in the world to come.	All sins shall be forgiven unto the sons of men, and blasphemies wherewith soever they shall blaspheme. But he that shall blaspheme against the Holy Ghost hath never forgiveness, but is in danger of eternal damnation.	And whosoever shall speak a word against the Son of man, it shall be forgiven him: but unto him that blasphemeth against the Holy Ghost it shall not be forgiven.

There is much common material here. All three accounts agree that to blaspheme against the Holy Spirit is to commit an unforgivable offence. Matthew and Luke agree that those who speak a word against the Son of Man can be forgiven; Mark and Matthew allow that sinners and blasphemers in general can be forgiven. If we allow that the substance of the accounts go back to an actual utterance of Jesus[51] the easiest way to understand the saying is in terms of the Jewish background to the Gospels. The *Damascus Document* from among the so-called Dead Sea Scrolls criticises the opponents of the Covenanters thus: 'they defile their holy spirit and open their mouth with a blaspheming tongue against

---

[51] Luz, *Matthäus* 1/ 2, p. 256, Fitzmyer, *Luke X – XXIV*, p. 962.

the laws of the Covenant of God.'[52] Evidence is provided by Strack-Billerbeck that in Rabbinic Judaism the Holy Spirit was understood as the Spirit of prophecy and inspiration, and that to speak against the Holy Spirit was to speak impudently against the Torah (i.e. the revealed laws and will of God), an offence that could not be forgiven.[53] Approached in this way, the saying is a warning to the opponents of Jesus that in denying that his works are the works of God, they are in danger of blaspheming against the Holy Spirit – the Holy Spirit understood as the inspirer of prophets and judges (see Judges 11.29). The references to the Son of Man in Matthew and Luke can be taken either to be the equivalent of Mark's 'sons of men' or Jesus's way of referring to himself. In the latter case, personal insults against his works of healing and exorcism cannot be forgiven, for they fail to recognise the activity of God.

The commentaries make it clear that later interpreters of the passage, and perhaps even the Gospel writers and the churches that they represented, read much more into the text than has been done here.[54] Perhaps the early church, seeing itself as the pre-eminent sphere of the Holy Spirit, epitomised the rejection of their message as a sin against the Holy Spirit. Another line of approach, found in Hebrews 6.4-6, was that the saying was a warning to Christians not to commit apostasy. The Hebrews passage mentions those who have become 'partakers of the Holy Ghost' and says that if they commit apostasy they cannot be restored to repentance.

---

[52] CD V. 11-12 in G. Vermes, *The Complete Dead Sea Scrolls in English*, London: Allen Lane, 1997, p.131; Hebrew text in E. Lohse, *Die Texte aus Qumran*, Munich: Kösel Verlag, 1964, p.74.

[53] H. L. Strack, P. Billerbeck, *Kommentar zum Neuen Testament aus Talmud und Midrasch*, Munich: C.H.Beck, vol. 1, 1926, p.637.

[54] See Luz, *Matthäus*, 1/ 2 pp. 263-268; Fitzmyer, *Luke X – XXIV*, pp. 964-5.

The implication of this line of approach is that the disciples who abandoned Jesus at his Passion could be forgiven and were forgiven (i.e. they committed a sin against the Son of Man), but after Pentecost and the outpouring of the Spirit, forgiveness for abandoning the faith could not be given.

Many interpreters have taken the substance of the saying to be that a person cannot be forgiven who refuses to accept that God is willing and able to forgive. Luz comments that as long as people are aware that they are sinners, they have not blasphemed against the Holy Spirit.[55] But he goes on to say that the idea of *unforgiveable* sin is hard to reconcile with the Gospel of the love of God, and that if called upon to preach about this part of the saying, he would have to preach *against* it. From the point of view of what is being argued in the present book, this saying about the Holy Spirit draws upon an Old Testament view of the Spirit, a subject to be discussed in a later chapter.

Other sayings about the Holy Spirit

(a) *Matthew 7.11 / Luke 11.13*

In Luke's version of the saying, Jesus says 'If ye then, being evil, know how to give good gifts unto your children; how much more shall your heavenly Father give the Holy Spirit to them that ask him?' However, where Luke has 'the Holy Spirit' Matthew has 'good things', and commentators are largely agreed that Luke has modified what was found in the source common to him and Matthew, and that 'good things' is closest to what Jesus said. [56]

---

[55] Luz, *Matthäus*, 1/ 2, p. 267.

[56] Fitzmyer, *Luke X – XXIV*, pp. 915-6.

(b) *Matthew 10.19-20 / Mark 13.11 / Luke 21.15*

Matthew 10.19-20	Mark 13.11	Luke 21.15
But when they deliver you up, take no thought how or what ye shall speak: for it shall be given you in that same hour what ye shall speak. For it is not ye that speak, but the Spirit of your Father which speaketh in you.	But when they shall lead you, and deliver you up, take no thought beforehand what ye shall speak, neither do ye premeditate; but whatsoever shall be given you in that hour, that speak ye; for it is not ye that speak, but the Holy Ghost	I will give you a Mouth and Wisdom which all your adversaries shall not be able to gainsay nor resist.

Although only Mark's account explicitly mentions the Holy Spirit, Matthew's 'Spirit of your Father' is close. Luke seems to imply that it will be Jesus himself who enables his disciples to defend themselves.[57] Mark and Luke agree in placing the saying in Jesus's discourse concerning the last times. Matthew places it in Jesus's mission charge to the disciples during his ministry. That the passages depend upon an authentic saying of Jesus seems clear, even if it is not possible to be sure of the occasion on which it was uttered.[58] Our concern here is to try to discover what is meant by the Holy Spirit in this passage. An approach via the Old Testament is suggested by Gnilka, and makes good sense.[59] He cites Exodus 4.15, where God assures Moses that he [God] will put into Aaron's mouth the words that need to be spoken. There are also assurances to prophets, who will face opposition, that God will assist their speaking (Jeremiah 1.6-9). Whether the saying is placed during the ministry of Jesus or

---

[57] See Barrett, *Holy Spirit*, p. 131.

[58] See Barrett, *Holy Spirit*, pp. 130-131.

[59] J. Gnilka, *Das Evangelium nach Markus*, p. 191.

42

it envisages the last times, it has an Old Testament flavour, a conclusion strengthened by Matthew's 'Spirit of your Father'.

(c) Matthew 28.18-20

The command of the Risen Lord to his disciples to baptise converts 'in the name of the Father, and of the Son, and of the Holy Spirit' is not regarded by critical scholars as an authentic saying of Jesus.[60] It is clear from the letters of Paul and the Acts of the Apostles that, according to the oldest baptism formulae, people were baptised in or into the name of the Lord Jesus (Acts 8.16) or into Christ Jesus (Romans 6.3). If Jesus had explicitly taught that a trinitarian baptismal formula was to be used, it is hard to explain why the first disciples deliberately used a different formula. The saying represents a stage of development of Christian thought where the full implications of the work and exaltation of Jesus were coming to be expressed in trinitarian language.

It should not be overlooked that, according to the saying, it is the Risen Jesus who will be 'with' his disciples until the end of the age. Whereas the Fourth Gospel speaks of Jesus breathing the Holy Spirit upon the disciples as he sends them out (John 20.21-2) and Luke describes the 'descent' of the Holy Spirit at Pentecost, Matthew is obstinately silent about the Holy Spirit's presence or work in the age of the Risen Lord.[61]

---

[60] See Barrett, *Holy Spirit*, p. 103.

[61] This point is emphasised by Luz, *Matthäus*, 1/ 4 (2002), p. 457.

The parables of Jesus

Nowhere in his teaching in Parables does Jesus mention the Holy Spirit. This accords with the scarcities of references to the Spirit in his teaching as a whole. It is arguable, however, that implicit in some of the Parables is the principle stated by Paul, that the letter kills but the Spirit gives life (2 Corinthians 3.6).

In the Parable of the Good Samaritan, the priest and the levite may have passed by the injured man because they were not generous-minded people, or because they were frightened that they, too, would become victims of the robbers if they stopped to give help. However, they may have passed by because they were frightened of becoming defiled by contact with a dead body.[62] Such defilement would render a person unclean (Numbers 19.11-13) and certainly prevent a priest or levite from officiating at the Temple for seven days, if they were on their way to Jerusalem for that purpose.[63] In this case, the observance of the letter of the law could have meant death for the injured man, if no one had stopped to help him. Samaritans accepted as authoritative law the five books of the Torah (i.e. Genesis to Deuteronomy) and thus the Samaritan who stopped to help was, in theory, bound by the same law of defilement as the priest and levite. He, being moved by compassion (Luke 10.33), acted according to the Spirit. His actions preserved the life of the injured man. Whether or not these considerations were in the mind of Jesus in telling the Parable, there is sufficient of a contrast in it between formal and generous

---

[62] See Fitzmyer, *Luke X – XXIV*, p. 887.

[63] Fitzmyer, *Luke X – XXIV*, p. 887 suggests that the priest was going home *after* serving in the Temple.

reactions to the plight of the victim to be able to see in it examples of the letter and the Spirit.

The same observation can be made about the Parable of the Labourers in the Vineyard (Matthew 20.1-16). If the owner of the vineyard had operated in accordance with the rules of fairness, the workers who worked only one hour would have received a twelfth of the wage of those who had done a full day's work. No doubt other considerations affected the owner's decision to pay all the workers the same wage, such as the fact that all had the same needs (e.g. to provide for their families) if not the same deserts. The owner's seemingly unfair action (unfair to those who had worked for twelve hours) can be seen as action prompted by the Spirit – driven not by deserts but needs.

Another Parable that can provoke strong reactions among modern readers is The Prodigal Son (Luke 15.11-32), where it seems to be grossly unfair that the brother who loyally served his father seems to come off worse than the brother who wasted his share of the inheritance. The behaviour of the father in welcoming the return of the Prodigal seems outrageous; and it is, if we live in a world governed only by the letter of the law. But there is the sphere of the Spirit, and this is undoubtedly what drives the action of the father.

The clash between the letter and the Spirit is clear, of course, in the disputes between Jesus and his opponents over the matter of observing the sabbath. The saying 'the sabbath was made for man, and not man for the sabbath' occurs at Mark 2.27 following the criticism of some Pharisees that the disciples of Jesus were defiling the sabbath by plucking and eating heads of grain on the sabbath.[64] What is striking in Mark's account is Jesus's reference to David's behaviour when he was on the run from Saul (1 Samuel 21.1-6, Hebrew 21.2-7) and obtained for his men and himself bread which could only be consumed by priests. What this example and the saying about the sabbath being made for man show, is that while rules are necessary to prevent human behaviour from being chaotic, they must not become ends in themselves. It is necessary to know when rules must be broken, and the breaking of rules belongs to the realm of the Spirit. It is creative and imaginative action, usually concerned with dealing with other people. It can be driven by compassion and by responding to people's needs, not their deserts. It is a supreme example of treating other people as ends, and not means.

Conclusion

Why did Jesus apparently say so little about the Holy Spirit during his earthly ministry? Why, given that the early church, as portrayed by the Acts of the Apostles and the letters of Paul, believed itself to be empowered by the Spirit, is there so little reference to the Spirit in the church's accounts of the life and ministry of its Founder? The first answer to these questions is historical. Jesus said little about the Holy Spirit, and this fact is faithfully portrayed in the Gospel records. Why did he say little? Here we enter the realm of speculation, but not without evidence. Barrett argues that, for Jesus, the coming of the Spirit in a way that took its activity and blessings beyond what was already found in the Old Testament, could happen only in the

---

[64] The incident is also recorded in Matthew 12.1-8 and Luke 6.1-5, without the saying that the sabbath was made for man. The relationship between the three accounts is complicated. See Luz, *Matthäus* 1/ 2, pp. 228-9.

Messianic Age, of which his ministry was the anticipation but not the fulfilment.[65] In this respect, the Holy Spirit was similar to the ideas of the Messiah and the Kingdom of God. The Kingdom was already operative in the ministry of Jesus but would only be fully established in the future by his Passion and Exaltation. The title 'Messiah' was avoided by Jesus because it belonged properly to a future age that was yet to be fully realised, and because it was open to considerable misunderstanding.

These conclusions have important implications for today's churches, especially those that do not display ostentatious signs of the work of the Spirit in their midst. If the ministry of Jesus was a remarkable testimony to the Spirit in the sense that his Parables and works of mercy were the very words and works of God reaching out to a fallen humanity, then any church that proclaims the words and works of Christ, and tries, however unsuccessfully, to live out their implications, is also being guided and empowered by the Spirit. Churches develop different kinds of ethos. I have attended services in many types of church in which it was difficult to connect what was taking place with the mission and message of Jesus as portrayed in the Gospels. I have experienced, less often than I would like, services that did seem to resonate with the simplicity of the life and words of Jesus. No doubt the Holy Spirit was active and present in all these different types of service, and it would be wrong to say that he was present in some and absent from others. We need to allow that the Spirit cannot be made to conform to our expectations of how and when he should act. This is why it is important to allow that lack of reference to the Spirit in the

---

[65] Barrett, *The Holy Spirit*, pp. 153-162.

ministry of Jesus did not mean that the Spirit was lacking. The same may be true of churches that do not make ostentatious reference to the Spirit.

CHAPTER 5

Paul and the Holy Spirit

Jesus said little about the Holy Spirit. Paul says much. There are more than fifty references to the Spirit or the Holy Spirit in the letters that are generally accepted as authentic. However, there is no systematic Pauline teaching on the subject. His allusions to the Holy Spirit were occasioned by his need to address particular problems. This chapter will therefore examine key passages in their contexts, and then try to draw together some kind of overview.

(a) Galatians 3.1-5

> O foolish Galatians! Who hath bewitched you, that ye should not obey the truth, before whose eyes Jesus Christ hath been evidently set forth, crucified among you? This only would I learn of you, Received ye the Spirit by works of the law, or by the hearing of faith? …having begun in the Spirit, are ye now made perfect by the flesh?…He that ministereth to you the Spirit, and worketh miracles among you, doeth he it by the works of the law, or by the hearing of faith?

Paul's opponents believed that Gentiles who became Christians should be circumcised and obey the law of Moses. This was not an unreasonable point of view for anyone who believed that Jesus was the Messiah and that he had fulfilled the Old Testament prophecies. For Paul, the event of Jesus Christ had radically altered the world. It had ushered in a new age, an age characterised by the outpouring of God's Spirit. This had radical implications for the observance of the law. Christians were not 'under' the law but were led by the Spirit.

Paul's words in Galatians 3.1-5 imply that something had happened that could be described as follows. The message of Christ crucified had been preached to them (Galatians 3.1) and they (or, perhaps, some, of the hearers) had been brought to faith in the Son of God who loved them and gave himself for them (Galatians 2.20). This brought a new awareness of God and of themselves in relation to God. It brought into being a fellowship or congregation which united together men and women, Jews and non-Jews, masters and slaves on a common basis – that God had accepted them all, for Christ's sake (see Galatians 3.28). In this new fellowship there was a sense of the presence of God's Spirit. It may have manifested itself partly by works of healing (the miracles referred to in verse 5), but also in the awareness of themselves as new people in a new relationship with God and with each other. Paul's point is that this new situation had come about because the gospel of Christ crucified had been preached, and hearers had come to faith. This could not have happened if they had been invited to be circumcised and to observe in some way the law of Moses. That path belonged to the old order, an order superceded by the death and exaltation of Jesus.

When Paul asks 'did you receive the Spirit?' he is not talking of individuals being endowed with some kind of life-enhancing power. He is talking of something corporate and communal – something shared, of course, by individuals, but a corporate awareness of living in a new age. This awareness was especially experienced and expressed in the worship of the congregation. Paul also asked whether, having begun with the Spirit, they would end with the flesh. This must lead to a consideration of another passage in Galatians.

(b) Galatians 5.16–24

> This I say then, Walk in the Spirit, and ye shall not fulfil the lust of the flesh. For the flesh lusteth against the Spirit, and the Spirit against the flesh; and these are contrary the one to the other; so that ye cannot do the things that ye would. But if ye be led by the Spirit ye are not under the law...the fruit of the spirit is love, joy, peace, longsuffering, gentleness, goodness, faith, meekness, temperance.

This passage has often been wrongly interpreted as though it were speaking of a struggle in the soul of individual believers between sinful desires (the flesh) and higher motives (the Spirit).[66] Things are not helped by translations such as the New English Bible, which renders the Greek word for flesh (*sarx*) as 'lower nature' or the Good News Bible which has 'human nature'. What is meant by 'flesh' here is a whole order of being, a sphere or dimension in which people have to live out their lives, and to which all, Christians and non-

---

[66] E .D. W. Burton, *The Epistle to the Galatians* (International Critical Commentary), Edinburgh: T & T. Clark, 1921, p. 300.

Christians alike, are to a greater or lesser extent in bondage.[67] If the flesh and the Spirit are in contention and opposition, this is not something that is taking place primarily *within* human beings (although it includes that); it is a cosmic struggle between all that is opposed to God (including fallen humanity) and God's realm, which is that of the Spirit. There is also an antithesis in the passage between the Spirit and the law. Law is necessary in a world in which the 'works of the flesh' are all too apparent. Law helps to restrain wickedness and to punish it. It does not abolish the 'works of the flesh' and has no power to produce 'love, joy and peace' (cp. Galatians 5.23). The summons to walk by or in the Spirit is a summons to follow a path or way. This way does not have to be pioneered anew by each believer; it already exists, its foundations having been laid by prophets and law-givers of the Old Testament, and its surface having been renewed by Jesus in the Holy Spirit. When Paul says that 'they that are Christ's have crucified the flesh with the affections and lusts' (Galatians 5.24) he is playing on the ambiguity of the word 'flesh'. To have crucified the flesh is not to have embarked upon a personal discipline of self-denial or rigorous moral reform; it is to have embraced Christian discipleship, living consciously in the sphere or dimension of what God has revealed of his love in Jesus Christ.

Only if we approach the passage in this way can we make sense of the fact that the 'fruit of the Spirit' is not a set of human achievements but the work of God's Spirit. No doubt there are people who are naturally more inclined to be generous, patient, faithful, and self-controlled than others.

---

[67] R. Bultmann, *Theologie des Neuen Testaments*, Tübingen: Mohr Siebeck, 1984 (9th ed). pp. 232-246, 336.

Perhaps, unbeknown to them, the Spirit is at work in their lives. At the end of the day, however, what is being described by the 'fruit of the Spirit' is the Kingdom of Right Relationships, a sphere made possible by God's incredible love and commitment to the human race. To walk in or by the Spirit is to live in this dimension of hope and forgiveness that God has made possible, as people steer their lives through the turbulent waters of the 'works of the flesh'.

(c) 1 Corinthians 12–14

The religious phenomenon of ecstatic utterance seems to be universal.[68] Paul himself claims to have 'spoken in tongues' (1 Corinthians 14.18) and wanted to encourage Corinthian Christians to do likewise (1 Corinthians 14.5). On the other hand, he was clear that even if the ability to 'speak in tongues' was a sign of the work of the Spirit, Paul regarded it as less important than other gifts of the Spirit. In chapter 13 he says explicitly that if he speaks in the tongues of men and of angels and lacks love (*agape*) then he is a noisy gong or a clanging cymbal (1 Corinthians 13.1). In chapter 14 he makes it clear that tongue-speaking is essentially something that occurs between an individual and God, and while it is valuable to this extent, it does not benefit the whole community. In chapter 12, Paul lists the utterance of wisdom and knowledge as workings of the Spirit, and among a series of questions which imply the answer 'no' Paul asks 'do all speak with tongues?'(1 Corinthians 12.30).

---

[68] R. Hempelmann, 'Zungenrede II' in *Theologische Realenzyklopädie*, 36, Berlin: de Gruyter, 2004, pp. 764-5.

In these chapters Paul links the work of the Holy Spirit to the Gospel of Jesus Christ. At 12.3 he writes that the confession 'Jesus is Lord' can only be made through the inspiration of the Spirit. In chapter 13, which describes the 'still more excellent way' of the higher gifts of the Spirit (1 Corinthians 12.31) in terms of love, the portrait on which he bases his description of love is surely drawn from Jesus of Nazareth.[69] Paul seems to have faced in Corinth a view of the Spirit that stressed the more spectacular manifestations of his presence, perhaps even to the extent that those who had certain gifts regarded themselves as superior to those who lacked them. Paul had no truck with such views. He stressed that there were many ways in which the Spirit worked in the Christian community and that the building up of the community was more important than the spiritual achievements of individual members. Ultimately, the purpose of the Spirit's work was to bear witness to Jesus, and to make the community Christ's body, harmoniously exercising differing gifts in the work of the Gospel.

(d) 2 Corinthians 3.1-18

Paul's opponents in Corinth had questioned his credentials as an apostle. In reply, Paul says that he needs no letters of commendation (for example, from the church in Jerusalem). His letter of recommendation is the fact of the existence of the church in Corinth, and it is a letter written not with ink or engraved upon stone, but written by the Spirit of God on the hearts of the Corinthian believers (2 Corinthians 3.1-3). The contrast between the letter written on material, and the letter written on human hearts enables Paul to speak of two

---

[69] C. K .Barrett, *The First Epistle to the Corinthians* (Black's New Testament Commentaries), London: A. & C. Black, 1968 , p. 310.

covenants: that of the written Old Testament law and that of the realm of the Spirit. Paul refers back explicitly to Exodus 34.29-35, according to which the face of Moses shone so brightly after he had been communing with God on the holy mountain, that he was obliged to veil his face when he came down from the mountain and spoke to the people. Moses had been receiving the written code from God. Using a form of argument familiar in Judaism, Paul argued that if the Mosaic dispensation was so glorious as to need Moses to veil his face, the dispensation of the Spirit must be even more glorious.

It is in this passage in 2 Corinthians 3 that Paul asserts that the letter (or the written code) kills, whereas the Spirit gives life. There also occurs an almost mystical passage in which Paul speaks of the transforming power of the Spirit. Drawing on the example of Moses whose face shone when he communed with God on the mountain, Paul claims that living in the sphere of the Spirit is like beholding God's glory, and that this has a transforming effect upon those involved. It also grants freedom to those involved. Their behaviour is not an anxious conformity to written laws, but a bold, creative and imaginative life lived in the hope and joy that the Spirit makes possible. The idea of the transformative effect of living in the sphere of the Spirit is similar to the description of the fruit of the Spirit in Galatians 5.22-3 which is the work of the Spirit in those who walk (i.e. live by and in) the Spirit.

(e) Romans 5-17, 26-7

This passage combines severity with tenderness. The severe words are in verses 5-8:

For they that are after the flesh do mind the things of the flesh; but they that are after the Spirit the things of the Spirit. For to be carnally minded is death; but to be spiritually minded is life and peace. Because the carnal mind is enmity against God; for it is not subject to the law of God, neither indeed can be.

As in Galatians 5.16-24, we are not dealing with the inner struggles of isolated individuals between good and evil. Flesh and spirit are two spheres or dimensions. 'Flesh' is the human realm and its structural arrangements that operate without regard to God. Those who live entirely within its domain live in the realm of death, because life is ultimately a gift of God and cannot be had apart from him. But this is not a state of affairs that God desires, and the opening verses of Romans 8 describe what God has done to end the power that 'the flesh' has over the human race. God sent his Son in the likeness of sinful flesh to fulfil its demands and to break its power. The death of Christ has created a new reality, that of the Spirit, where Jesus is acknowledged as Lord, and where people live with a new awareness of themselves in relation to God and to others. The exclusivist tone of verses 5 – 8 emphasises that it is not a matter of indifference whether people belong to the flesh or the Spirit. To use an analogy, if a part of a town was about to be flooded and a boat was standing by to take those threatened by the flooding to safety, we would not think that harsh language was out of place when it was explained what would happen to those who chose not to embark.

The tender words come in verses 26-27:

Likewise the Spirit also helpeth our infirmities; for we know not what we should pray for as we ought; but the Spirit itself maketh intercession for us with groanings that cannot be uttered, And he that searcheth the hearts knoweth what is the mind of the Spirit, because he maketh intercession for the saints according to the will of God.

Two things stand out in this passage. First, the Spirit is spoken of in personal terms. If, in the earlier verses of the chapter, the Spirit is a sphere or dimension opposed to 'the flesh', here the Spirit is personal, aware of, and entering into human weakness and uncertainty. To be 'in the Spirit', therefore, is to have an awareness that God is meeting us at those most personal and vulnerable points of our human lives. The stress on human weakness is the second important point. It is all too easy to associate the work of the Holy Spirit with manifestations of power, such as 'speaking in tongues' or claimed extraordinary instances of physical healing. Here, however, it is the work of the Holy Spirit not to manifest power, but to meet believers in their weaknesses. To know that one is weak, and to believe that God's Spirit is present at that weakness is to be as strong as if spectacular spiritual things were happening (cp. 2 Corinthians 12.10).

The tender tone of Romans 8 is also to be found in verses 9 - 17. Paul says that Christ is 'in' believers, and that although their bodies are dead because of sin, their spirits are alive because of righteousness. The Spirit that raised Christ from the dead gives life to believers because it dwells in them (Romans 8.10-11). What does this mean? In what sense is Christ 'in' believers, and how does the Holy Spirit 'dwell' within them? Paul may be alluding to Genesis 2.7, where God breathed the breath of life into the dust, in order to create a living being.[70] In this case there will be an analogy.

---

[70] The Hebrew for breath of life is *nishmat haiim* and does not use the usual Hebrew word for Spirit, namely, *ruach*.

The difference between physical life and death is breath (i.e. the ability to breathe). The difference between spiritual life and death is the Holy Spirit. The main point of the analogy is not *where* breath or the Holy Spirit are to be located in the human body, but the fact that both are a gift from God. To say that Christ is 'in' believers and that the Holy Spirit 'dwells' within them is the language of metaphor and not to be taken literally. It is probably easier for modern readers to think in terms of the influence and inspiration that come to us from others, as set out in the perceptive essay by Cyril Emmet. [71] The matter is further spelled out in verses 14-17.

> For as many as are led by the Spirit of God, they are the sons of God. For ye have not received the spirit of bondage again to fear; but ye have received the Spirit of adoption, whereby we cry Abba! Father. The Spirit itself beareth witness with our spirit, that we are the children of God: And if children, then heirs; heirs of God, and joint heirs with Christ.

Here again the Spirit is described in personal terms, and not in connection with his *location* within believers, but according to his *function* or working. To come to the awareness that the Son of God loved us and gave himself for us (Galatians 2.20) is the work of the Holy Spirit. It is a gift of the Spirit, and begins a commitment of the Spirit to sustain us in the new awareness that he has made possible. Part of the way in which the awareness is sustained and believers walk in the Spirit is through the worship of the Christian community and participation in its mission. Barrett suggests that the

---

[71] C. Emmet, 'The Psychology of Grace: How God Helps' in Streeter. *The Spirit*, pp. 159-195.

words 'when we cry "Abba! Father" ' allude to Christian worship, and the use of the Lord's Prayer in worship.[72]

(f) 1 Corinthians 3.16, 6.19

> Know ye not that ye are the temple of God, and that the Spirit of God dwelleth in you? .... Know ye not that your body is the temple of the Holy Ghost which is in you, which ye have of God?

These two sayings evidently refer respectively to a corporate 'dwelling' of the Holy Spirit, and an individual one.[73] The corporate sense is easier to understand than the individual sense. The Christian community, as a visible and active manifestation of the body of Christ, is where the Spirit is active. Indeed, it is probably more accurate to say that the Christian community lives its life in the larger dimension of the Spirit, rather than that the Spirit comes to take up residence in the Christian community. Barrett refers to Hellenistic writers for whom the idea was not uncommon, that God dwelt not in buildings made of stone, but in human hearts.[74] No doubt it was easier for people in the ancient world to make sense of the idea of the spirit 'dwelling' in individuals than it is for readers today, for whom such language must be metaphorical. Perhaps a way of understanding the metaphor is to think of the individual's participation in the Spirit (in the sense of the dimension created by God in the death and exaltation of Jesus) rather than the Spirit's 'presence' in the individual. What must be

---

[72] C. K. Barrett, *The Epistle to the Romans* (Black's New Testament Commentaries), London: A. & C. Black, 1962, pp.163-4.

[73] See Barrett, *First Epistle to the Corinthians*, pp. 90,151. J .A. T. Robinson, *The Body. A Study in Pauline Theology*, London: SCM Press, 1957, p.64, appears to treat both passages as referring to a corporate 'indwelling' of the Spirit.

[74] Barrett, *The First Epistle to the Corinthians*, p. 90.

avoided is language that is *impersonal*. The 'dwelling' of the Holy Spirit in individuals must mean that people are aware of the working of the Spirit in their lives, for example in guidance, and in helping them to see inadequacies which they are led to place before God in prayer. To say that an individual is a temple of the Holy Spirit is to say that his or her life is one in which Jesus is Lord. In some traditional Christian teaching the verses under consideration have been interpreted in a narrow, sexual way, and have caused much anxiety to people who have felt obliged to strive for unrealistic ideals of sexual abstinence, lest they defile their body where the Holy Spirit 'dwells'. It is true that in 1 Corinthians 6.12-20 Paul is warning his readers against immorality; but what he seems to have had in view was behaviour that was inconsistent with living in the dimension of the Spirit rather than the need for constant striving for unrealistic standards of chastity.

Conclusion

In trying to sum up Paul's teaching on the Holy Spirit I intend to use the analogy, suggested by Emmet, of an orchestra and its conductor.[75] An orchestra, founded by its conductor, is an entity to which musicians can belong. It is personal, in the sense that it would not exist but for its conductor-founder, and in that it is directed by the conductor, who has invited players to become members, knows their particular talents, and welds them into a harmonious whole. Each musician makes a unique contribution and at the same time is enriched by experiencing what the whole orchestra achieves. The analogy of the orchestra enables the Spirit to be conceived as a dimension into which people are

---

[75] C. W. Emmet, 'Psychology of Grace' p. 161.

invited. It exists *before* players become members. The analogy also preserves the personal aspect. The Spirit is like the conductor, who interacts personally with the musicians.

All analogies have weaknesses, of course, and are often as useful at the points at which they fail as at the points where they are illuminating. The analogy of the orchestra does not explain that the orchestra exists to oppose a realm of human activity that is heedless of God and therefore destructive to humanity. It does not illuminate the fact that the realm of the Spirit is established by the death and exaltation of Jesus because it is opposed to the realm that is heedless of God. It does, on the other hand, emphasise that although the realm of the Spirit exists as something into which people are invited, it is also to some extent constituted by those who have accepted the invitation. What they do together under the guidance of the Spirit enriches them as individual members, and makes more effective the action of the whole body. Another important aspect *not* illustrated by the orchestra analogy is that of weakness. Players will not be invited into the orchestra unless they are top-class musicians. There are no such conditions attached to entry into the realm of the Spirit. Rather, membership is most likely to depend upon a recognition of personal weakness and unworthiness in the presence of God, and of God's astonishing readiness to accept and forgive anyone who believes that this is what God is like.

CHAPTER 6

The Spirit in the Fourth Gospel

In the Fourth Gospel the references to the Holy Spirit are more in terms of a *person* than anywhere else in the New Testament. This is especially the case in the Farewell Discourses of chapters 14 and 16. It is essential for Jesus to depart from his disciples, otherwise the Paraclete (also called 'the Spirit of truth' at John 16.13) will not come to them, sent by the Father (John 14.26) and Jesus himself (John 16.7). How to translate the Greek word *parakletos* is a difficult matter, and English versions use such renderings as 'Comforter', 'Counsellor', 'Advocate' and 'Helper'. The view taken here is that 'Advocate' is the best rendering, for several reasons.

First, the Greek word had become a loan-word in the Aramaic and Hebrew of the beginning of the Common Era. It has the sense of 'mediator' in the Targum (Aramaic paraphrase) to Job 33.23, and 'intercessor' in the Babylonian

Talmud.[76] A close equivalent is found in the New Testament in I John 2.1-2, 'if any man sin, we have an advocate (Greek *parakleton*) with the Father, Jesus Christ the righteous'. Second, the Spirit is given an adversarial function in John 16.8-11:

> And when he is come, he will reprove the world of sin, and of righteousness, and of judgment: Of sin, because they believe not on me; Of righteousness, because I go to my Father, and ye see me no more; Of judgment, because the prince of this world is judged.

Third, the rendering 'Advocate' has a two-way reference lacking in the words 'Comforter', 'Counsellor' and 'Helper'. Those latter words imply that the Spirit is 'given' to assist the disciples. This is true; but the Spirit is also 'given' to bear witness to Jesus – to who he is and what he has done – and 'Advocate' can convey this sense as well as the sense of assisting the disciples. The 'Advocate' can also be seen as an interpreter, something implied in John 16.8.

Oliver Quick has written that

> the meaning of the revelation [of the Godhead in the incarnate Word] could not be grasped in any full way until the Paraclete had come to enable those who had already believed on Jesus to know him truly. And this gift of the Spirit could not be bestowed until Jesus had been glorified on the cross and gone back to the Father. Not until then could the disciples be in Christ and he in them, as all along Christ had been in the Father and the Father in him.[77]

---

[76] *Shabbat* 32a, 'when one ascends the scaffold to be put to death, if he has prominent intercessors (Hebrew *peraqlitin*) he is pardoned'. *Baba Bathra* 10a R. Eleazar b. R. Jose [c. AD 180] said 'all acts of charity are great peace[makers] and intercessors (Hebrew *peraqlitin)* between Israel and his Father in heaven'.

[77] O. C. Quick, *Doctrines of the Creed. Their Basis in Scripture and Their Meaning Today*, London: Nisbet & Co., 1938, pp. 289-90.

This quotation not only makes much sense of the teaching about the Holy Spirit in John 14 and 16, but of passages elsewhere in the Fourth Gospel.

(a) John 1. 32-34

In the account of the baptism of Jesus in John 1.32-4, John the Baptist is given the following words:

> I saw the Spirit descending from heaven like a dove, and it abode upon him. And I knew him not; but he that sent me to baptize with water, the same said unto me, Upon whom thou shalt see the Spirit descending, and remaining on him, the same is he which baptizeth with the Holy Ghost. And I saw, and bare record that this is the Son of God.

The writer of the Fourth Gospel uses the 'witness' of John the Baptist to express his own theology. Basing himself on the tradition in the first three Gospels that Jesus saw the Spirit descending dove-like upon him (only in John 1.33 is this seen by someone other than Jesus) he makes John the Baptist witness, not that Jesus is a charismatic or Spirit-filled person, but that he is the Son of God. Further, the Spirit in the passage has an interpretative role. It was only because John the Baptist saw the descent of the Spirit that he understood who Jesus really was. Ahead of the glorification of Jesus on the cross, John the Baptist is enabled, by seeing the descent of the Spirit, to interpret correctly that Jesus is the Lamb of God (John 1.36).

(b) John 3. 1-11

The second passage dealing with the Holy Spirit occurs in John 3.1-11. Nicodemus comes to see Jesus because he is impressed by the signs (i.e. miracles) that Jesus performs. The reply of Jesus is, in effect, that he is not merely a teacher sent from God, but something or someone greater. However, this is something that can be understood only by those who are 'born from above', that is, those to whom understanding is given by God. Entrance to the kingdom of God is by water and the Spirit. Here, the Fourth Evangelist looks forward to the post-Resurrection era in which baptism by water following on from faith made possible by the Holy Spirit enables believers to become members of the church. However, the analogy between understanding something or someone in a radically new way, and new birth, is an appropriate one. In comparing the unfathomable (from a human standpoint) workings of the Spirit with the wind, whose effects can be seen but not the wind itself, the narrative is exploiting the fact that the Hebrew word *ruach* can mean both wind and Spirit (see Ezekiel 37.1-10). The issue is not whether Jesus is a teacher sent from God, but whether he is the Son of God whom God sends into the world in order to save it (John 3.16). Only the Spirit can disclose this; miracles do not.

At the end of John 3 is a further brief reference to the Spirit in verse 34:

> For he whom God hath sent speaketh the words of God:
> for God giveth not the Spirit by measure unto him.

The words 'not...by measure' mean that God's endowment of Jesus with the Spirit is limitless, so that the words that Jesus speaks are always also the words of God.[78]

---

[78] A. T. Lincoln, *The Gospel According to St. John* (Black's New Testament Commentaries), London: Continuum, 2005, pp. 162-3.

(c) John 7. 37-39

> In the last day, that great day of the feast, Jesus stood and
> cried, saying, If any man thirst, let him come unto me and
> drink. He that believeth on me, as the scripture hath said,
> out of his belly shall flow rivers of living water. (But this
> spake he of the Spirit, which they that believe on him
> should receive: for the Holy Ghost was not yet given; be-
> cause Jesus was not yet glorified.)

The easiest part of this saying is the end. Although Jesus is
limitlessly endowed with the Holy Spirit, this will not be
apparent until he is glorified, and only then will the Spirit be
available for those who believe. The difficulty in the saying
lies in locating the passage from which the quoted scripture
comes, and in punctuating and interpreting the Greek of
verses 37-8.[79] There is, in fact, no known passage in the Old
Testament from which the scripture citation can have been
taken. Instead, there are various passages that speak of life-
giving water: water flowing from a rock (Exodus 17.1-7),
from the visionary restored Temple (Ezekiel 47.1-12) or
simply Jerusalem (Zechariah 14.8). What is important for the
present work is the clear link between the glorification of
Jesus and the bestowal of the Spirit upon those who believe
in him.

(d) John 20.21-23

> Then said Jesus to them again, Peace be unto you: as my
> Father hath sent me, even so send I you. And when he had
> said this, he breathed on them, and saith unto them, Re-
> ceive ye the Holy Ghost: Whose soever sins ye remit, they

---

[79] For a full discussion see Lincoln, *The Gospel According to St. John*, pp. 254-7.

are remitted unto them; and whose soever sins ye retain, they are retained.'

The Fourth Gospel gives an alternative view of the timing of the post-Resurrection bestowing of the Holy Spirit compared with Luke/Acts. If the writer(s) of this Gospel was familiar with Luke/Acts it is interesting that an alternative view was given. However, it is entirely consistent with the theology of the Spirit in the Fourth Gospel. Jesus has been glorified in his death and resurrection. The Spirit can now be given to his followers, as promised in John 14 and 16. The Spirit is given by Jesus himself, to enable the disciples to continue the task for which Jesus was sent by the Father. The breathing upon the disciples is presumably an allusion to Genesis 2.7 where God breathes the breath of life (Hebrew *nishmat haaim*) into the dust from which mankind is made.

It is most unfortunate that in the history of the church's use of this passage it has been restricted so as not to apply to all believers. In the 16th century Ordinal of the Church of England, which was used until the latter part of the last century, the passage was used at the ordination of priests, and was held to give them authority to pronounce the Absolution in divine worship, because of verse 23. In doing so it drew upon earlier precedents.[80] This is not the place to discuss the nature and authority of the priesthood; the present book is concerned with the interpretation of the Bible. Whatever the Church has made of this passage rightly or wrongly, in the context of Johannine theology it has to be allowed that the gift of the Holy Spirit was intended for all believers

---

[80] See F. Proctor, W. H. Frere, *A New History of The Book of Common Prayer. With a Rationale of its Offices*, London: Macmillan, 1905 (3rd ed), p 660

(John 7.38) following the glorification of Jesus, and not simply for a small group within the company of believers.

What, then, is meant by the authority (if that is what it is) to forgive and retain sins? If the task of the Spirit is to bear witness to Jesus and his saving work, and if this has the effect that people respond positively or negatively (see John 3.18-21) then sins will be forgiven or retained. The sacerdotal use of the passage reduces the Spirit to a power conveyed to and upon the disciples gathered in the Upper Room (minus Thomas). In the context of the Fourth Gospel it must be seen as the fulfilment of the promises made earlier in the book, that the Holy Spirit will make possible for all believers an encounter with the glorified Jesus, and will continue the work that Jesus was sent by the Father to accomplish.

CHAPTER 7

The Holy Spirit in the Acts

It has already been pointed out that the New Testament has at least three views of what happened after the resurrection of Jesus. According to Matthew 28, Jesus appeared to the disciples in Galilee and commissioned them to preach and baptise. He promised to be with them until the end of the age. There is no mention of the giving of the Holy Spirit. In John, the Holy Spirit is breathed upon the Apostles (minus Thomas) on the first Easter Day. In Acts, the Holy Spirit descends upon the disciples on the day of Pentecost, that is, on the fiftieth day after Passover, and thus roughly seven weeks after the resurrection.

The account of the giving of the Holy Spirit to the church most familiar to churchgoers is that in Acts. As the Christian liturgical calendar developed, the timetable of Luke/Acts was followed, giving the now familiar pattern of five Sundays after Easter, Ascension Day on the Thursday after the Fifth Sunday (approximating to the forty days of Jesus's appearances according to Acts 1.3) and Pentecost or Whitsunday ten days after Ascension Day. It is most unfortunate that things should have developed in this way because of all the books of the New Testament, Acts portrays the Holy Spirit almost (but not entirely) exclusively as a *power* rather than a *person*.

What is the origin of the Acts account of the Day of Pentecost? We cannot rule out the possibility that at some point after the resurrection (not necessarily fifty days later) a group of disciples in prayer and discussion were illuminated in a remarkable way by God's Spirit and saw in this event a new beginning in their corporate experience. An oral tradition of this could be the basis for the Acts narrative. Various attempts have been made to see in Acts 2.1-13 an allusion or allusions to Old Testament passages and Jewish interpretation of them. Thus, the account of the scattering of the human race and the proliferation of languages in Genesis 11.1-9 has been seen to be reversed by the fact that the Jews present at the festival in Jerusalem hear the apostles speaking in languages that each nationality can understand. There are at least two difficulties with this suggestion. The first is that the difference of languages is *reinforced* not reversed (i.e. it is not the case that a universal language understood by all replaces the individual languages). Second, all those attending the festival are presumably Jews or Jewish proselytes (i.e. converts or would-be converts to Judaism) and hardly representative of ethnic diversity.[81] Another suggestion is to

---

[81] C. K. Barrett, *The Acts of the Apostles* (International Critical Commentary), Edinburgh: T. & T. Clark, vol.1, 1994, pp. 118-120 fully discusses the problems arising from the list of nationalities in Acts 2.8-11 and the fact that they are present at a *Jewish* festival.

link the Pentecost narrative with the Jewish tradition that at the Feast of Weeks (i.e. Pentecost) the divine Torah was given to Israel. The link would mean that on the Day of Pentecost, God's new law was revealed to the church. However, Barrett thinks that this, and related ideas in Judaism, are too late to be a source for the Acts narrative.[82]

The problem of the narrative for modern readers is that the idea that the Holy Spirit can enable people to speak foreign languages that they have never studied is both alien to their experience, and the cause of a good deal of mischief. One has heard anecdotes about unbelieving professors of ancient languages going accidentally or unwillingly to Pentecostal churches, at which they hear someone speaking perfect ancient Egyptian, for example. The present writer was once asked to give an opinion on whether some words spoken by a worshipper were biblical Hebrew. They were not. Such stories, and the fact that people believe them to be true, do nothing to help churchgoers understand the nature and work of the Holy Spirit. I am not aware that there is any validated instance of a missionary *not* needing to learn the language of the people to whom he or she was sent, because the Holy Spirit would automatically enable them to speak that language. We have to be frank about the Acts account of the Day of Pentecost. It may be based upon a memory of a defining moment in the disciples' understanding of the significance of the death and resurrection of Jesus, and it may have been accompanied by the ecstatic language that we know was practised in the church in Corinth. The view that these were *foreign* languages immediately recognisable by native speakers of various nationalities, is not historically

---

[82] Barrett, *Acts*, vol.1, p. 111.

true. It is a theological interpretation designed to show the universal significance of the death and resurrection of Jesus (see Acts 1.8). The account of the spread of the Gospel from Jerusalem to Samaria (Acts 8) and to the Gentiles (Acts 10), and through the Pauline mission then illustrates this point.

If the Holy Spirit is seen in Acts primarily as a *power*, it can also be said that it is because it picks up an element of the very diverse treatment of the Spirit in the Old Testament. In Acts 1.16-20 the Holy Spirit is described as the inspiration that enabled David in Psalms 69.25 and 109.8 to prophesy that Judas would betray Jesus.[83] Again, in Peter's speech in Acts 2 the prophecy of Joel is quoted, that God will pour out his Spirit (Joel 2.28-32a, Hebrew Joel 3.1-5a; Acts 2. 17-21), and it is claimed that this is what had happened on the Day of Pentecost (Acts 2.33) because of the death and resurrection of Jesus. Towards the end of his speech Peter promises that those who repent and are baptised will receive the gift of the Holy Spirit (Acts 2.38). In Acts 4.8 Peter is filled with the Holy Spirit when he explains to the high-priestly family the name and power in which a lame man has been healed (Acts 4.8). This, again, presents the Holy Spirit as prophetic inspiration, as do verses 25 and 31 in Acts 4.

A new viewpoint is found in Acts 5 in the story of Ananias and Sapphira (Acts 5.1-11), who attempt to deceive Peter and the apostles by claiming to give them the whole proceeds of the sale of property while actually retaining some of the proceeds for their own use. Peter accuses the couple of lying to the Holy Spirit, of lying to God, and of tempting the Spirit

---

[83] See Barrett *Acts*, vol. 1 pp. 100-101 for a discussion of the relationship between the Acts version of these quotations and those in the Hebrew and Greek Old Testaments.

of the Lord (Acts 5.3-4,9). While the interpretation of verses 3-4 and how they relate together is not straightforward[84] the Holy Spirit is clearly seen in *personal* terms. Whether this is also the case in Acts 6.3 and 5, where the seven men who are to be chosen as 'deacons' are to be full of the Holy Spirit is hard to say. Most likely they are to display those works and signs that indicate the indwelling *power* of the Spirit. If Stephen's accusation in Acts 7.51 that the Israelites resisted the Holy Spirit is an allusion to Isaiah 63.10 ('they rebelled and grieved his holy Spirit'[85]) this, again, picks up an Old Testament theme.

The problem of Acts 8, where the 'giving' of the Holy Spirit is restricted to the laying on of hands of the apostles but denied to Philip (one of the 'deacons') has been discussed in chapter 2, where the view was taken that this chapter (and Acts 19.1-7) was primarily about the orderly and authorised expansion of the church. It was also noted in earlier chapters how the Holy Spirit in Acts, through prophetic inspiration, initiated the missionary work of Saul and Barnabas in the church in Antioch, and also directed its course (Acts 13.1-2, 16.6-7). It is not necessary to discuss these matters, nor the remainder of Acts, further.

Conclusion

The Acts of the Apostles has played a predominant role in shaping the understanding of the Holy Spirit among church-goers. It has determined the liturgical calendar, with Pentecost or Whitsunday being the 'birthday' of the church. It has justified the view that the Holy Spirit is a power or gift that

---

[84] See the discussion in Barrett, *Acts*, vol. 1, pp. 266-7.

[85] See Barrett, *Acts*, vol.1, p.376.

can be 'conveyed' when authorised persons (bishops or elders) lay hands upon believers. It has fostered the false view that the Holy Spirit enables people to speak foreign languages that they have never studied. It has emphasised the view that the presence of the Holy Spirit is indicated by spectacular manifestations such as ecstatic utterances or miraculous healings.

While there is no desire in the present book to deny that God is able to do remarkable things through his Spirit, his active presence in the world, there is a desire to direct believers to other parts of the Bible from which they can gain a more rounded and comprehensive view of the Holy Spirit and his work. Acts emphasises the remarkable and spectacular aspects of the Holy Spirit. This is not the whole story, as I hope the earlier chapters have made clear.

CHAPTER 8

The Holy Spirit in other parts of the New Testament

Of the books of the New Testament not dealt with in the earlier chapters, it is the Revelation of St John the Divine that contains the most interesting material on the Holy Spirit. In particular, there are two important themes: the messages of the Spirit to the seven churches, and the visionary experience of being 'in the Spirit'.

In each of the seven letters to the seven churches the formula is used 'he that hath an ear, let him hear what the Spirit saith unto the churches' (Revelation 2.7, 11, 17, 29; 3.6, 13, 22). The Spirit here is clearly not a power; he is personal. Perhaps it is no accident that the formula resembles what comes in Mark 4.9 at the end of the Parable of the Sower, 'he that hath ears to hear, let him hear'. Certainly, the sender of the letters to the church is the glorified Christ seen by the author of

Revelation in his inaugural vision (Revelation 2.1,12,18; 3.1,7,14). The phrase 'let him hear what the Spirit saith to the churches' can presumably only mean that Christ and the Spirit are identified in the way in which the Spirit is promised in John 14.25, 16.13-15[86]. What Revelation 2 - 3 conveys is a vivid sense of the concern of the glorified Christ that his followers should be warned against false doctrines and should be encouraged to overcome the spiritual and other forces ranged against them. The writer may well have been a Christian prophet, but not one prophesying in the way that occurred in the church in Corinth (1 Corinthians 14.5). The book of Revelation is elaborately structured and draws on literary and oral traditions. The view of the Holy Spirit that is implied is complex and composite. It combines the Spirit of Old Testament prophecy with the New Testament function of bearing witness to what God has done in Jesus Christ. It fulfils the promises found in the Fourth Gospel that Jesus will send another Paraclete (John 16.7) and it anticipates later theology in which Jesus and the Spirit are 'persons' of the undivided Trinity. For modern church-goers these chapters are a reassurance and a reminder that their local congregations are not merely the sociological equivalents of voluntary associations. They are Christ's people brought into being by what God has done in Christ, and watched over by the glorified Christ through his Spirit.

The other distinctive emphasis in Revelation is the phrase 'in the Spirit' in Revelation 1.10, 4.2. This recalls Old Testament passages such as Ezekiel 2.2; 3.12,14, where the Spirit enters into the prophet and takes him to places to behold things

---

[86] T. Holtz, *Die Offenbarung des Johannes* (Das Neue Testament Deutsch), Göttingen: Vandenhoeck & Ruprecht, 2008, p. 34.

about which he will write. However, its probable nearest equivalent is in 2 Corinthians 12.1-4, although the word 'Spirit' does not occur there. This is Paul's account of a 'man in Christ', almost certainly himself, being caught up into the third heaven and hearing things that could not be told. What is being described there and in Revelation is a visionary experience in which, whether in a trance or with enhanced normal faculties, a participant is admitted to an apprehension of realities which, while exceeding the bounds of normal understanding, have to be described in images drawn from the normal world, even if they are used in unusual and bizarre ways. This is something experienced rarely, by few people, and not confined to Christians, although any authentic Christian mystical experience will be centred upon Christ, as in the book of Revelation.

An important different emphasis is found in Ephesians 1.13 - 14, which in turn is probably dependent upon 2 Corinthians 1.21-22.

2 Corinthians 1.21-22	Ephesians 1.13-14
Now he that stablisheth us with you in Christ, and hath anointed us, is God; Who hath also sealed us, and given the earnest of his Spirit in our hearts.	In whom also, after that ye believed, ye were sealed with that holy Spirit of promise, Which is the earnest of our inheritance.

It will be noticed that the Ephesians passage seems to simplify that in 2 Corinthians. The latter implies two actions: sealing, and giving the Holy Spirit, the Ephesians version implies one action, namely sealing with the Holy Spirit. In both passages the word rendered 'earnest' is the Greek *arrabon* meaning pledge, or first instalment. The commentators[87] point out the commercial aspects of the notion of sealing, i.e. identifying property or documents in order to establish ownership or prevent forgery. Helpful as this is, it tends to depersonalise the Holy Spirit, especially in the Ephesians version of the passage. A seal is a *thing*, and the question is raised as to how God does the sealing with the Holy Spirit. Is it through baptism, or laying on of hands? Justification for taking a different approach is offered by Ephesians 4.30:

> And grieve not the holy Spirit of God, whereby ye are sealed unto the day of redemption.

Clearly, one cannot grieve a *thing*, and the verse articulates a strongly personal idea of the Spirit. A possible way of making sense of this for modern churchgoers is by the analogy of friendship. A friendship can promise much for the future. It can mark a possession in the sense that friendship can bring with it mutual obligations. To be sealed in or with the Holy Spirit can be explained as follows using the analogy of friendship. God invites us into friendship through the preaching of the Gospel and our response to it. We receive a new awareness of ourselves in relation to God. This is the work of the Holy Spirit, i.e. God in action. The fact that God is for us marks us out as his possession (see also Romans 8.31-39). But the friendship is incomplete because we are mortal creatures of time and space. From God's side the friendship is complete, and a guarantee of things to come. We can develop the analogy of friendship further by noting that friendships are often sealed by gifts, or by frequent actions such as texting, exchanging cards and

---

[87] For example C. K. Barrett, *The Second Epistle to the Corinthians* (Black's New Testament Commentaries), London: A. & C. Black, 1973, p.79-80; A. T. Lincoln, *Ephesians* (Word Bible Commentary), Dallas: Word Books, 1990, pp. 39-41.

giving presents. One way of describing baptism is to say that the use of water represents God's outward sign of friendship. We can then say that the Holy Spirit is not so much 'given' but that his friendship and abiding presence are 'sealed' (i.e. demonstrated) by the visible actions of baptising. It also needs to be said that friendship with God can only be initiated from his side. We can no more approach God and invite his friendship than we could do this with a member of the Royal Family. And the friendship which God offers is much more astonishing than any human friendship could be. Towards the end of Revelation 1 the seer, having seen the glorified Lord, falls at his feet as though dead (Revelation 1.17). This is the one whose friendship is offered, and made real in the Holy Spirit.

1 John 5.6-9

This passage is a famous crux in the textual criticism of the New Testament, which can be best illustrated by comparing the passage in the Authorized and Revised Versions.

Authorized Version	Revised Version
This is he that came by water and blood, even Jesus Christ; not by water only, but by water and blood. And it is the Spirit that beareth witness, because the Spirit is truth. For there are three that bear record in heaven, the Father, the Word and the Holy Ghost; and these three are one. And there are three that bear witness in earth, the Spirit, and the water, and the blood: and these three agree in one.	This is he that came by water and blood, even Jesus Christ; not with the water only, but with the water and with the blood. And it is the Spirit that beareth witness, because the Spirit is the truth. For there are three who bear witness, the Spirit, and the water, and the blood: and the three agree in one.

The reasons for the differences are well explained in the standard commentaries and ultimately do not affect the interpretation of the passage for present purposes. The immediate question is what is meant by water and blood. Various suggestions have been made: that they refer to the blood and water that issued from the side of Jesus when it was pierced by a Roman spear (John 19.34-5) or that the water refers to John 7.38 where Jesus links the giving of the Spirit to water that will flow from the hearts of believers. The view taken here is that the water refers to the baptism of Jesus and the blood to his crucifixion. These two events span his public ministry. The role of the Spirit can be related to John 1.32-4 where John the Baptist understands that Jesus is the Son of God because he sees the descent of the Spirit upon Jesus. In other words, without the illumination of the Holy Spirit the baptism and passion of Jesus are merely things that happened to someone who lived 2,000 years ago. The illumination of the Spirit enables believers to understand that these events show who Jesus was: the Son of God, through whom God was reconciling the world to himself (2 Corinthians 5.19). C. H. Dodd[88] makes the important point that the witness of the Holy Spirit to the meaning of the ministry of Jesus is not merely confined to the past, and he suggests that in the sacraments of Baptism and Eucharist we have counterparts to water and blood which re-present the objective facts of the ministry of Jesus in the life of the church. The Holy Spirit enables these 'visible words' to become the means of grace within the church, and witnesses to their truth.

---

[88] C. H. Dodd, *The Johannine Epistles* (The Moffatt New Testament Commentary), London: Hodder and Stoughton, 1946, pp. 130-131.

CHAPTER 9

The Spirit in the Old Testament

It is usual in books on the Holy Spirit that deal with the biblical material to begin with the Old Testament. This procedure is deliberately not followed in the present work. What the Old Testament says about the Spirit is many-sided, and there is also the fact that there are definite developments in the way in which the Spirit is written about. For example, the prophets of the 8th and 7th centuries are virtually silent about the Spirit of God. The majority of references are to be found in material that is post-exilic (i.e. later that the 6th century B.C.). There is also the fact that the Hebrew word normally translated as Spirit or spirit *(ruach)* plays an important part in describing human moods, feelings, passions and intellectual and cultural abilities. Any chapter on the Spirit in the Old Testament is bound to be complex; and to have such a chapter at the beginning of a book may deter some readers from going any further.

The treatment of the Spirit in the Old Testament is in fact more far-reaching than in the New Testament, and in some cases it supplies answers to unanswered questions in the New Testament. It is hoped that the placing of the chapter towards the end of the present work will enable it to be more useful than if it was regarded merely as an introduction to what was to come in the New Testament, or merely as 'background'. The present chapter is entitled 'The Spirit in the Old Testament' for the reason that the phrase 'Holy Spirit' occurs only three times in the Old Testament. The occurrences are Psalm 51.11 (Hebrew 51.13) 'take not thy holy Spirit from me', Isaiah 63.10 'but they rebelled and vexed his holy Spirit' and Isaiah 63.11 'where is he that put his holy Spirit within him?' These, and other passages, will be considered in detail later in the chapter.

The Spirit as expressing human moods, feelings, passions and intellectual and cultural abilities

Any way of talking about inner moods and feelings has to draw upon concrete metaphors. In English we speak of being heart broken, or having a lump in the throat, a shiver down the spine or the hair standing on end, none of which expressions are to be taken literally. In Hebrew, the word *ruach*, spirit, is used in similar ways.[89] In Genesis 26.35, where Esau has married two Hittite women we read that the two women 'were a grief of mind' to Esau's parents, Isaac and Rebekah.' Revised Standard Version 'they made life

---

[89] There is a useful summary in the section ' "Ruach" as a Psychological Term to denote dominant disposition' in N. H. Snaith, *The Distinctive Ideas of the Old Testament*, London: Epworth Press, 1944, pp. 146-150.

bitter' gives completely the wrong sense. What the phrase means is that Isaac and Rebekah felt inwardly distressed because of Esau's choice of foreign women as wives. It does not mean that the two wives made life difficult for their parents-in-law. The word *ruach* (spirit) here means an in-ward disposition that could be upset by unfortunate circumstances.

In Numbers 5.11-28 an ordeal is described to which a husband can subject his wife if he suspects, but cannot prove, that she has been unfaithful to him. Verse 14 speaks of the 'spirit of jealousy' coming upon him. We have only to reflect upon our own feelings, and how jealousy can flare up in our hearts and minds, to see this as a description of a human emotion or disposition.[90] At Exodus 6.9 the people refuse to listen to Moses because of their 'anguish of spirit' which probably means impatience, and not 'broken spirit' as in the Revised Standard Version.

In 1 Samuel 1.15, the distressed Hannah, who is praying to God at the sanctuary of Shiloh, is accused by Eli the priest of being drunk. She replies that she is of 'a sorrowful spirit' (literally 'hard of spirit').[91]

Several Hebrew words, meaning crushed (*dakka*), lowly (*shephal*), dim or faint (*kehah*) are used with *ruach* to express the ideas of being crushed, broken, or disheartened (and

---

[90] Against Snaith, *Distinctive Ideas*, p.146, who seems to think in terms of an irresistible external invading force.

[91] Because this phrase occurs only here in the Bible in Hebrew, and seems to mean obstinate rather than troubled, some commentators read 'day' (*yom*) instead of spirit (*ruach*) with the Greek. A 'hard day' would be a hard time. However the context makes it clear that if the traditional Hebrew text is correct, it must mean 'troubled in spirit' rather than obstinate. See S.R.Driver, *Notes on the Hebrew Text and the Topography of the Books of Samuel*, Oxford: Clarendon Press, 1913 (2nd ed.), p.14.

note the presence of the word 'heart' in the English word!). See, for example, Isaiah 57.15 'I dwell in the high and holy place, with him also that is of a contrite (*dakka*) and humble (*shephal*) spirit' and Isaiah 61.3 'the garment of praise for the spirit of heaviness (*kehah*)'. On the other hand, the word *ruach* is used to describe haughty and sexually impulsive behaviour. Hosea 4.12 (also 5.4) speaks of the spirit of harlotry (*zenunim*) that has led Israel astray, while Proverbs 16.18 mentions a 'haughty spirit' (*govah ruach*), literally, a lofty or tall spirit, that goes before a fall. Zechariah 12.10 speaks of a spirit of compassion (*hen*) and supplication (*tahanunim*) that will be engendered in those who 'look on him whom they have pierced'. [92]

In Daniel 2.3, King Nebuchadnezzar announces that he has had a dream, as a result of which his 'spirit is troubled to know the dream'. The Hebrew verb translated 'troubled' (*pa'am*) here in the passive, means to strike or impel. The same phrase occurs at Genesis 41.8, where the Pharaoh is troubled by his dream about the seven fat and seven gaunt cows. A person's spirit can be 'hot' (Ezekiel 3.14; 'I went in the heat [*hemat*] of my spirit') and 'cool' (Proverbs 17.27: 'a man of understanding is of an excellent spirit' [Hebrew *qar ruach* – cool of spirit]). A person's spirit can also be moved or stirred to do something generous. At Exodus 35.21 when gifts are needed for the building of the tabernacle in the wilderness, contributions are made by those 'whose spirit moved' them. The Hebrew verb translated as 'moved' is *nadav*, which has the sense of to volunteer, offer freely. This verse also mentions those whose heart was stirred, a re-

---

[92] There is no agreed interpretation regarding who it is who has been pierced, and the traditional Hebrew text has 'they will look on me'. See J. W. Rogerson 'Zechariah' in J. D. G. Dunn, J. W. Rogerson (eds.) *Eerdmans Commentary on the Bible*, Grand Rapids: Eerdmans, 2003, p. 727.

minder that words other than *ruach* are used in biblical Hebrew to describe emotions and behaviour. The term *ruach* can also mean something like the English 'character' or 'disposition'. At Numbers 14.24, where God has decreed that none of those whom he brought up out of Egypt will reach the promised land because of their refusal to trust him, an exception is made for Caleb 'because he had another spirit with him (literally 'there was a different spirit with him') and hath followed me fully'. The same is found in Psalm 32.2 where the man is called 'blessed' in whose spirit (i.e. character) there is no deceit (*remiyyah*).

An important passage is Isaiah 11.2, where it is said of the one who will come from the root of Jesse that

> the Spirit of the LORD shall rest upon him,
> the spirit of wisdom and understanding,
> the spirit of counsel and might,
> the spirit of knowledge and the fear of the LORD.

Should the translation of the Hebrew be 'the spirit' or 'a spirit'?[93] How is the notoriously difficult genitive relationship (indicated by 'of' in the English) to be translated or understood?[94] The Good News Bible, employing Nida's transformational approach has the following rendering of the verse:

> The Spirit of the LORD will give him wisdom,
> and the knowledge and skill to rule his people.
> He will know the LORD's will and honour him.

---

[93] See A.R. Johnson, *The Vitality of the Individual in the Thought of Ancient Israel*, Cardiff: University of Wales Press, 1964 (2nd ed.) p.34 and the New English Bible for the rendering 'a spirit...' etc.

[94] See E.A. Nida, *Toward a Science of Translating, with Special Reference to Principles and Procedures involved in Biblical Translating*, Leiden: E.J.Brill, 1964, pp. 64-5.

What the translators have done here is to transform the noun phrases such as 'spirit of wisdom' into verbal statements, 'spirit that gives wisdom', and they have also been treated as explanatory genitives, e.g. 'spirit that consists of knowledge and skill, etc.'[95] When these questions have been raised, others remain. Is the text speaking here of a supernatural endowment, not merely the enhancing of innate powers,[96] or is the promised leader one who will be endowed with outstanding gifts from and because of his birth? Does the passage say anything about *God's* spirit? These questions must remain unanswered for the moment. Whatever the answers, the passage clearly associates the *ruach* in at least one human being with the exercise of wisdom, knowledge and discernment.

So far in this section it has been demonstrated that the Hebrew writers referred to had a sophisticated understanding of human nature. They knew that people were defined by their character; that people could be jealous or generous, patient or impatient. They knew that people could be haughty or humble, and that circumstances could crush their outlook on life and rob it of hope. They knew that there were gifted people in the field of wisdom, knowledge and instruction. All these aspects of human nature were described with the help of the word *ruach*, as well as with other words such as *lev* (heart).

---

[95] See A.B. Davidson, *Hebrew Syntax*, Edinburgh: T.& T.Clark 1901 (3rd ed.), p.33; G.B.Gray, *The Book of Isaiah* (International Critical Commentary), I – XXVII, Edinburgh: T.& T.Clark 1912, p.216 'The spirit of Yahweh settles upon the King as a *spirit of*, or, as we should say, imparting, *wisdom and discernment.'*

[96] See B. Duhm, *Das Buch Jesaia*, Göttingen: Vandenhoeck & Ruprescht, 1922 (4th ed.), p. 105.

It would be surprising if these facts were irrelevant when the question is considered as to what the Hebrew writers meant when they used the word *ruach* in relation to God. Yet discussions of the *ruach* of God often begin from the fact that the word can mean wind. H. W. Robinson writes that 'in the fundamental Hebrew usage… it (*ruach*) denoted a wind-like energy'.[97] Although he goes on to say that later the word (*ruach*) comes to denote 'his (man's) whole psychical life' little or no use is made of this fact in the remainder of his book. From a different perspective, the interesting sections in Snaith and Johnson[98] tend to play down the sophisticated way in which *ruach* is used with regard to human nature in favour of the Spirit of God as an invading, irresistible force, closer to the energy of wind than a profound understanding of human emotions. In what follows here the view will be taken that while there are no doubt passages in the Old Testament that explain the fact that *ruach* means 'wind', it is also necessary to pay attention to the uses of the word that describe human emotions. This is one of those areas in which the Old Testament has much more to say, and much more to offer, than the New Testament. (Other areas include prayer, doubt, suffering and theodicy.) It would be a pity if this sophistication were to be overlooked in an examination of the Holy Spirit because there was a presumption that what the Old Testament had to say on the matter was essentially rudimentary, and even primitive. However, the next section will discuss those passages in the Old Testament in which the *ruach* of God is an expression of his power.

---

[97] H.W.Robinson, *The Christian Experience of the Holy Spirit*, London: Collins, Fontana Books, 1962, p. 25.

[98] Snaith, *Distinctive Ideas*, pp.143-158; Johnson, *Vitality*, pp. 22-37.

The *ruach* of God as God's power

In the story of the plagues, the Exodus and the wilderness wanderings, winds sent by God play a part in assisting the escape of the Hebrews from Egypt, their crossing of the Red Sea, and their being sustained in the wilderness. Thus an east wind from God brings the plague of locusts upon Egypt, and a west wind removes them when they have consumed everything (Exodus 10,13,19). When the Hebrews are caught between the Red Sea and the pursuing Egyptian army, God drives the sea back by means of a strong east wind so that the Hebrews can cross to the other side (Exodus 14.21). In order to feed the Hebrews in the wilderness God provides a wind that diverts quails into the path of the travellers (Numbers 11.31). These winds are not fortuitous, from the point of view of the biblical writers. They are the means by which God personally intervenes in order to rescue and sustain his people. The winds embody God's presence and action.

In the story of Jonah the wind is used in order to ensure that God's plans and will are carried out. A great wind is hurled by God against the ship in which Jonah is trying to escape from going to Nineveh (Jonah 1.2). This forces the mariners to throw Jonah overboard in order to save the ship and themselves. At the end of the book God uses 'a sultry east wind' to afflict Jonah after the destruction of the castor oil plant that has been sheltering him from the sun (Jonah 4.8). This enables God to teach Jonah about the divine concern for plants and animals as well as people.

It is along similar lines that those passages should be understood that speak of the way in which God's spirit rapidly transports people from one place to another. In 1 Kings 18.7 -

16, when Obadiah unexpectedly meets Elijah during the severe drought, Obadiah complains that if he tells King Ahab that he has met the prophet and Ahab then tries to find him, Obadiah will be killed by the king because the Spirit of the LORD will have carried Elijah 'whither he knows not', and Ahab will not be able to find him. At 2 Kings 2.16 some of the 'sons of the prophets' suggest to Elisha that a search party should be sent out to look for Elijah in case the Spirit of the LORD has caught him up and taken him to a mountain or valley. Elisha knows that such a search will be pointless, because he saw Elijah being taken up into heaven. The prophet Ezekiel finds that the Spirit lifts him up and takes him to where the exiles are to be found, in Telabib near the river Chebar in Babylon. (Ezekiel 3.12,14; 8.3, 11.14.) What these passages have in common with those about God's use of the wind to bring plagues and storms, is that they describe God's interaction with the world of human affairs. However, it should not be thought that 'ordinary Israelites' expected miraculous things to happen when they felt or heard the wind, or that they expected the wind suddenly to transport them somewhere. We are dealing with *narratives* that are stating that the world of the biblical writers was one in which God was believed to be present and active, and mention of the wind and Spirit were ways of conveying that belief.

It is now necessary to examine those passages in which, according to some scholars, the Spirit of God 'rushed' upon certain individuals. This view is most apparent in the New Revised Standard Version. The Spirit 'rushes' upon Samson when he is confronted by a young lion (Judges 14.6), when he is out-riddled by the men of Ashkelon (Judges 14.10) and when he is handed over to the Philistines (Judges 15.14). At 1

Samuel 10.6 and 10.10 the same Hebrew word verb as in the Judges passages *(tsalach)* is translated by the NRSV as 'possess' in connection with Saul's meeting of a band of ecstatic prophets and in 1 Samuel 11.6 the NRSV translation of this verb is 'came upon'. However, an evil spirit from God (which will be discussed later) 'rushes' upon Saul, according to 1 Samuel 18.10. Three questions need to be answered. Does the Hebrew verb *tsalach* mean 'to rush'? Second, how does it differ in meaning from passages which, in Hebrew, say that the Spirit 'was upon' certain people. Third, how are we to understand what the passages are saying about the Spirit and its operation?

The justification for translating *tsalach* as 'rush' is that this is the meaning given in the authoritative Hebrew lexicon of Brown, Driver and Briggs.[99] However, no support for this meaning is cited from other Semitic languages (the same verbal stem in Syriac is quoted as meaning 'cleave', 'penetrate', 'advance') and the only two occurrences in contexts other than endowment by the Spirit (Amos 5.6 and 2 Samuel 19.18) are considered by the lexicon to be dubious (i.e. that the Hebrew text has been corrupted in the copying process). Further, Hebrew lexicons prior to that of Brown, Driver and Briggs do not give 'rush' as the meaning of *tsalach*. [100] Also, translations of the verb are not consistent. It is used of what happened to David after he had been anointed by Samuel, and the NRSV here has 'came mightily upon' rather than

---

[99] F. Brown, S. R. Driver , C.A. Briggs, *A Hebrew and English Lexicon of the Old Testament*, Oxford: Clarendon Press, 1906, p. 852.

[100] See, for example, Gibbs's translation of the Gesenius lexicon: J. W. Gibbs, *A Hebrew and English Lexicon to the Old Testament... from the German Works of Gesenius*, London: Howell and Stewart, 1837, where the meaning 'to fall upon' is given; also J. Fuerst, *A Hebrew and Chaldee Lexicon to the Old Testament*, (trans. S. Davidson), London: Williams and Norgate, 1867 (3rd. ed.), p.1191, where the meaning is given as 'to cut into one, i.e. to press violently upon him'. It must be allowed that it is not easy to see the connection between 'cut into' and 'press violently'.

'rushed' (1 Samuel 16.13). This passage is important because while a case could be made for the Spirit coming in a violent way upon Samson when he was provoked or in danger, this sense hardly fits the case of David after Samuel anoints him. It has to be questioned seriously whether 'rush' or some similar notion is the proper rendering of *tsalach*.

In the book of Judges, in addition to the use of *tsalach*, the verb 'to be' (*hayah*) is found in connection with the Spirit. In Judges 3.9-10 God raises up Othniel to save the Israelites and the Spirit 'came upon him'. The Hebrew is literally 'was upon him'. Similarly, when Jephthah sets out on his campaign to deliver the people the Spirit 'comes upon him' (Hebrew *hayah*). In 1 Samuel the evil Spirit that comes upon Saul is prefaced by both verbs: in 1 Samuel 18.10 it is *tsalach*, (NRSV 'an evil spirit ... rushed upon Saul') in 1 Samuel 19.9 it is *hayah* (NRSV 'an evil spirit ... came upon Saul'). I conclude that there are no grounds for translating *tsalach* as 'rushed' or even 'came mightily upon'. If we are to be guided by the fact that *hayah* (to be) and *tsalach* seem to be interchangeable, we must avoid translations that suggest violent or mighty sudden endowment with the Spirit. On the ground that the verb *tsalach* seems, in related Semitic languages, to mean 'cleave' (in the sense of 'split'), 'penetrate', 'advance' we might tentatively suggest 'enter' for *tsalach* in connection with the Spirit. The verb is usually used with the preposition *'al*, usually rendered as 'upon'. The rendering 'entered upon' would be unusual use of English, but retains the sense that the Spirit came from outside the person who was endowed.

How are we to think of the process of the Spirit entering or being upon a person? Are the texts speaking of something entirely irrational in the sense that persons who are endowed contribute nothing to the actions they perform under the inspiration of the Spirit? When Samson confronts the young lion do his sense of self-preservation and his courage make no contribution to his response? When deliverer-judges such as Othniel (Judges 3.10), Gideon (Judges 6.34) and Jephthah (Judges 11.29) are inspired by the Spirit, do their sense of crisis, their courage, their gifts as leaders make no contribution to the deliverance they achieve? If the answer to these questions is that their various gifts and abilities must have counted for something, another factor has to be considered. Are the texts that speak of the Spirit of God less concerned with the 'how' of the means of endowment, and more with signalling that God was at work in various individuals, graciously redeeming his people through their deeds? If the answer to this question is 'yes', then texts that speak of the Spirit being 'with' certain individuals have the same function as those that describe God using the wind to drive back the Red Sea, feed the Israelites in the wilderness with quails, and wreck the boat in which Jonah is trying to escape from his commission. This function is to describe a world in which God is present and active, using the forces of nature, and the natural instincts, emotions and intellectual gifts of individuals to accomplish his plans. With these points in mind the chapter will now examine a number of key passages.

(a) Genesis 1.2
'the Spirit of God was moving over the face of the waters'
This verse has generated an enormous amount of discussion, and has divided Bible translators. The NRSV renders the phrase 'a wind from God swept over the face of the waters'. There are two arguments used to justify the rendering 'wind'

rather than 'Spirit'. The first is that in other ancient cosmologies in Babylonian and Egyptian texts, a wind is one of the elements present in the chaos before the world is created.[101] However, scholars are far from agreed as to whether such parallels support the case for the rendering 'wind' in Genesis 1.2. The second argument is that the Hebrew word *elohim*, usually translated as God or gods, can be used to express a superlative. The classic example is at Genesis 23.6 where the Hittites say to Abraham 'you are a mighty prince among us' and the Hebrew is literally 'a prince of God' (*elohim*). This argument justifies the rendering 'mighty wind' found in the New English Bible.

The view taken here is that the biblical writers, assuming that they were familiar with Babylonian or Egyptian cosmologies, which is far from certain, are as likely to have wanted to disagree with them as to copy them. Second, the combination of *ruach* with *elohim* never has the sense of a 'mighty wind' anywhere else in the Bible in Hebrew, and is unlikely to do so here. The more likely sense is that while the world was created by God imposing order upon an undifferentiated mass of material, he was present from the very beginning before the order was imposed. The Spirit of God is the presence of God. The verb translated as 'moved' is *merahephet* used at Deuteronomy 32.11 of a bird hovering or fluttering over its young. It is to be doubted whether the NRSV 'swept' can be justified. On the analogy with Deuteronomy 32.11, the Spirit of God in Genesis 1.2 has a guarding or caring sense, looking forward to what is to be created. It is the introduction to the many instances in the Old Testament

---

[101] See the detailed discussion by M. DeRoche, 'The *ruah elohim* in Gen 1.2c: Creation or Chaos?' in Eslinger and Taylor, *Ascribe to the Lord*, pp. 303-318.

when the Spirit of God will be the active presence of God in human affairs and occurrences in the natural world.

(b) Numbers 11.10-30

In this incident, Moses complains to God that he finds the task of leading the Israelites in the wilderness too difficult to cope with on his own. God tells him to select seventy men and to bring them to the tent of meeting, where God will come to them, and put upon them some of the Spirit that rests upon Moses. This Moses does. God takes some of the Spirit that is on Moses and puts it upon the assembled elders. According to the usual translations (e.g. RSV, NRSV)

> when the spirit rested upon them, they prophesied. But they did so no more.

However, there are two named persons, Eldad and Medad, who are not present in the tent of meeting. The Spirit rests upon them also, and they prophesy. Joshua appeals to Moses to forbid them. Moses refuses to do so, and expresses the wish that the whole people might be prophets, and that the Spirit might rest upon all of them.

The episode raises many difficult questions, not least the problem that the seventy elders who are given the Spirit in order to assist Moses in his work do not appear again in the narrative, and Moses apparently continues to carry the burden alone! There is also a question of the Hebrew text and translation at Numbers 11.25. The version quoted above, 'they did so no more', is based upon the traditional Hebrew text. However, two ancient versions, the Aramaic Targum and the Latin Vulgate, vocalise the Hebrew text to yield the meaning 'they did not cease [to do so]' and this is followed, among others, by Noth and Seebass.[102] For present purposes the main question is that of the function of the Spirit in the episode. The view taken here is that it is a legitimating device, and that the main point of the narrative is to argue that 'prophecy' can and should operate outside institutional channels. Joshua, in the narrative, represents the institutional view that prophecy should be controlled by institutions such as the Temple (which is represented in the narrative by the tent of meeting). Eldad and Medad represent prophets who operate outside the organised cult.[103] This implies that the 'prophesying' referred to is not the ecstatic behaviour associated with Saul and the prophets (1 Samuel 10.10-12) but prophetic speaking. As Seebass notes[104] ecstatic behaviour would hardly help Moses to administer the care of the people, and does not fit with Deuteronomy 18.15 where Moses is described as a prophet. The episode seems to be a narrative that reflects a struggle between institutional religion and groups insisting on the right to speak in God's name outside and against the institution. Lohfink cites the struggles of Jeremiah against part of the establishment.[105] The Spirit in the narrative is thus not to be thought of as expressing 'primitive' ideas. The Spirit functions as a device to legitimise prophecy that is exercised outside of institutional boundaries. To this extent, the episode has a message for today's church.

---

[102] M. Noth, *Das vierte Buch Mose: Numeri* (Das Alte Testament Deutsch), Göttingen: Vandenhoeck & Ruprecht, 1966, p.74; H. Seebass, *Numeri* (Biblischer Kommentar Altes Testament IV/2), Neukirchen-Vluyn: Neukirchener Verlag, 2003, p. 31. The difference is between *yasaphu* from *yasaph*, 'to do again' and *yasuphu* from *suph* 'to cease'.

[103] This interpretation is indebted to N. Lohfink, 'Charisma. Von der Last der Propheten' in *Unserer großen Wörter. Das Alte Testament zu Themen dieser Jahre*, Freiburg: Herder Verlag, 1977, pp. 241-251.

[104] Seebass, *Numeri*, p.31

[105] Lohfink, 'Charisma', pp. 245-251.

(c) 1 Samuel 19.18-24

This is a narrative in which the Hebrew verb 'to prophesy' (*nba* in the Hithpael) must mean to be seized by ecstatic behaviour. David is on the run from Saul and seeks the protection of Samuel at Ramah. When Saul's servants arrive to arrest David, Samuel is presiding over a group of ecstatic prophets. The Spirit of God comes also upon Saul's servants. They fall into ecstasy and cannot carry out Saul's orders. Two further groups of servants sent by Saul suffer the same fate until finally, Saul himself arrives and is also overwhelmed by the Spirit of God. He strips off his clothes, 'prophesies', and lies naked for the rest of the day and night. This gives rise to the proverb 'Is Saul also among the prophets?'[106] The important question is how far the view of the Spirit of God found in this narrative, i.e. that it overpowers people and renders them incapable of rational action, can or should be applied to other passages in the Old Testament. The safest answer is that this should be determined by the context. For example, it is likely that the other passages in which the proverb 'Is Saul also among the prophets?' is found (1 Samuel 10.11-12) also refers to ecstatic (i.e. irrational) prophecy. This is unlikely, however, in Numbers 11.16-29, in spite of Noth's assertion that the 'prophesying' referred to in Numbers 11 should be understood in the light of 1 Samuel 10 and 19.[107] As was pointed out above such activity would hardly help Moses to bear the burden of administration of the people.

---

[106] For a detailed discussion of this proverb in its earlier occurrence at 1 Samuel 10.11-12 see W. Dietrich, *Samuel* (Biblischer Kommentar Altes Testament VIII), Neukircher-Vluyn: Neukirchener Verlag, 2010, pp. 437-9.

[107] M.Noth, *Numeri*, p. 79.

In the incident in 2 Kings 3.15-19 when Elisha asks for a minstrel to play for him so that the hand of the LORD comes upon him (there is no mention of the Spirit or prophecy) the result is not ecstasy, as in 1 Samuel 10.5 where the prophets play musical instruments, presumably to inspire their ecstasy, but clear instructions to the Kings of Israel, Judah and Edom on how to conduct their attack upon Moab. No doubt the tendency of older scholarship to read into passages about prophecy the idea that it was ecstatic and irrational was driven by the conviction that ancient Israelites were 'primitive' in their conception of these matters. This cannot be taken for granted, and should be resisted wherever possible.

(d) 1 Samuel 16.13-23, 17.10-12

These are very difficult, but important, passages. In 1 Samuel 16.13 David is anointed by Samuel and the Spirit of the LORD comes (Hebrew verb *tsalach*) upon David 'from that day forward'. It is to be noted that the verb *tsalach* here cannot mean a sudden and temporary eruption of the Spirit. It must refer to a permanent endowment. Because the LORD's Spirit has departed from Saul, Saul is troubled by an evil spirit from the LORD. This evil spirit which troubles Saul (1 Samuel 16.15-16) can be soothed by music, which is one reason why David is introduced into Saul's household. He is a skilled musician, and his playing helps to make the evil spirit depart (1 Samuel 16.23). On one particular occasion the evil spirit comes upon Saul (Hebrew verb *tsalach)* and he 'prophesies', an action which takes the form of trying to kill David by casting a spear at him (1 Samuel 18.10-12). The context in this case makes it clear that the 'prophesying' is irrational.

It is tempting to explain the incidents by saying that Saul was suffering from depression and that the 'Hebrew mind' understood this in terms of an evil spirit sent from God.[108] There may be some truth in this; but it is necessary to go deeper. It has been argued earlier that the Old Testament use of the notion of spirit to describe human passions, emotions, and intellectual gifts is very sophisticated. The jealous husband who suspects his wife's infidelity in Numbers 5.14 is not said to be afflicted by an evil spirit from the Lord, but to be driven by a human spirit of jealousy. Thus, Saul could have been simply humanly jealous of David without God's involvement; except that he is the king on whose success or failure the very survival of the people of God depends.

Within the narrative complex of the stories of Saul and David, it is David who must succeed, because only so will the people of God overcome the threat posed to their existence by the Philistines. The evil Spirit from the Lord is not simply a Hebrew way of describing what we would call jealousy and depression. It is also a way of saying that God is actively involved in the affairs of his people and, if necessary, will frustrate leaders whose continued leadership will bring disaster. This introduces a problem for modern readers. Would God do such a thing? Would he send an evil spirit to frustrate a leader? However, this in turn raises the question as to how far we can create God in our own image and expect him to act only in ways that meet with our approval. The Book of Job tackles this question head on when the friends of Job deny God by defending him in rational terms, while Job, who complains bitterly about and

---

[108] See, for example, P. R. Ackroyd, *The First Book of Samuel* (Cambridge Bible Commentary). Cambridge: Cambridge University Press, 1971, p. 135.

to God, is vindicated.[109] Uncomfortable as the idea might be of God sending an evil spirit upon a leader, it expresses the idea that God's active presence and work in the world (his Spirit) go beyond the bounds of human reason and expectations, as God plans and wills salvation for the human race.

(e) 1 Kings 22.1-28

In this episode the king of Israel, Ahab, and his vassal Jehoshaphat king of Judah, are preparing to fight the king of Syria in order to re-take possession of the town of Ramoth-gilead. They seek, and get, a favourable forecast from the four hundred or so prophets who are connected in some way with the royal court in Samaria. Jehoshaphat is not satisfied and asks whether there is besides a prophet of the LORD who can be consulted. This seems to imply that the four hundred may not be 'prophets of the LORD' although their message is that 'the LORD shall deliver it [Ramoth-gilead] into the hand of the king' (see 1 Kings 22.6-7). Ahab realises that there is such a prophet, Micaiah son of Imlah, who has the disadvantage that he only prophesies evil about Ahab. Micaiah is summoned and confirms the favourable pronouncement of the other prophets. Presumably, he does so in a way that arouses Ahab's suspicion, for he charges Micaiah to tell the truth. The truth is that Micaiah 'saw all Israel scattered upon the mountains, as sheep that have no shepherd' (verse 17), that is to say, he saw Ahab killed and his army defeated. Micaiah justifies the conflict between him and the other prophets by relating a vision in which he saw God surrounded by the heavenly host and seeking for a

---

[109] See W. Dietrich, C. Link, *Die Dunklen Seiten Gottes*, vol.2. *Allmacht und Ohnmacht*, Neukirchen-Vluyn: Neukirchener Verlag, 2000, pp.70-74 for a treatment of 1 Samuel 16.14 similar to that offered here, and pp. 85-90 for a similar treatment of Job.

volunteer to entice Ahab to his death. A spirit[110] comes forward and says that he will be a lying spirit in the mouths of the prophets who forecast victory for Ahab. In this way, Ahab will be encouraged to fight a battle in which he will lose his life. Ahab orders that Micaiah should be imprisoned and starved until the king returns in peace from the battle. Micaiah's rejoinder is that if Ahab does return, then the Lord will not have spoken through him [Micaiah].

The episode is interesting in at least two respects. First, it personifies a spirit who is given a mission to lead the prophets astray. Second, verse 23 claims that God has put a lying spirit in the mouth of the prophets who forecast victory for Ahab.

The narrative must be understood in a way similar to that in 1 Samuel that speaks of the evil spirit that troubles Saul. The lying spirit is a narrative device that shows that God is sovereign over human affairs as he exercises judgement. 1 Kings 21 has related Ahab's arrogance and lawlessness in his illegal seizure of Naboth's vineyard. God's judgement is carried out in chapter 22 by means of Ahab's death in a battle about whose outcome God has deliberately misled him. Modern readers will find this idea difficult, preferring to live with a sanitised view of God; but they have to ask themselves this: do they want to live in a world in which injustice is ignored? Do they want a God who is indifferent to the deeds of tyrants such as Ahab? If their answer is 'no' then they should find some hope in this episode. If the narrative has a moral difficulty it is not that God has misled

---

[110] Hebrew 'The spirit' but this is a case where the definite article in Hebrew must be rendered by the indefinite article in English. See Davidson, *Hebrew Syntax*, p.26 (e).

prophets. It is that in going to war Ahab will cause the deaths of soldiers on both sides, soldiers who are merely the tools of the selfish ambitions of their leaders. But this is something that we can easily come to terms with in a world in which western civilised powers intervene in order to impose regime changes upon less-enlightened peoples, with many thousands of innocent people suffering in the process.

(f) Psalm 51.10-12 (Hebrew 12-14)

> Make me a clean heart, O God,
> and renew a right spirit within me.
> Cast me not away from thy presence,
> and take not thy holy Spirit from me.
> O give me the comfort of thy help again
> and stablish me with thy free Spirit.

The phrase translated here in the Book of Common Prayer as 'a right spirit' presents the difficulty that *ruach* is normally feminine in Hebrew, whereas the word following it is masculine and, if it is an adjective, should be in the feminine form. But if *nakhon* is a noun meaning 'a just man', and not an adjective meaning 'just' or 'steadfast' the translation 'spirit of a just (or upright) man' is what is needed. 'Spirit' will refer to a particular kind of character, as elsewhere. The verb rendered 'create' is *bara*, the verb used in Genesis 1.1 for God creating the universe. The psalmist's use of this verb expresses his awareness of a need for total dependence upon God.

The passage contains one of the few references to 'holy Spirit' in the Old Testament. It is clear from the parallelism of the Hebrew poetry that the phrase 'holy Spirit' is here equivalent to God's presence, the Hebrew literally meaning 'do not send me away from before your face'. The second part of the verse will mean something like 'do not take from me your presence'. The Hebrew is literally 'the Spirit of your holiness' which probably means something like 'the Spirit that belongs only and properly to you, God'.

The last phrase 'stablish me with thy free Spirit' (here, the adjective 'free' has the feminine form!) raises the question whether it is the psalmist's spirit or God's Spirit that is referred to. A case can be made for either, but preference is given here for the reference to be to God's Spirit. The psalmist in verses 11-12 (Hebrew 13-14) asks God always to be present with him and for that abiding presence to be willing on God's part. It will be in this confidence and assurance that he will be able to teach God's ways to those who rebel against God (verse 13, Hebrew 15).

(g) Isaiah 63.10-14

> But they rebelled and vexed his holy Spirit;
> Therefore he was turned to be their enemy,
> and he fought against them.
> Then he remembered the days of old,
> Moses and his people, saying,
> Where is he that brought them up out of the sea
> With the shepherd of his flock?
> Where is he that put his holy Spirit within him?
> That led him by the right hand of Moses with his glorious arm,
> dividing the water before them,
> To make himself an everlasting name?
> That led them through the deep
> as an horse in the wilderness, that they should not stumble?
> As a beast that goeth down into the valley,
> the Spirit of the LORD caused him to rest.

There are three references in this passage to the Spirit of God, two of them combined with the word 'holy'. The complete passage is Isaiah 63.7-14, which Westermann has convincingly compared with the 'historical' psalms, i.e., psalms such as Psalm 78, which are extended meditations upon God's dealings with his people as remembered in the traditions.[111] The importance of this comparison is that the Isaiah passage uses the idea of the Spirit of God to indicate God's personal and compassionate guiding of his people in the remembered events. In this context the reference to the people rebelling against and grieving God's holy Spirit may indicate an awesome dimension within the idea of God's Spirit. God's Spirit is not a benevolent aspect of God that is indifferent to whether or not people respond to his grace and mercy. God's Spirit has a 'dark' side which, if necessary, will change God from being a friend to being an enemy, if being an enemy is necessary to maintain God's relationship with his people and to accomplish the divine purposes. In this case, the Hebrew phrase *ruach qodshō*, literally, 'the spirit of his holiness' will mean something like 'the Spirit that upholds the holiness of God'. This is perhaps a more pro-found notion than anything that occurs in the New Testament. The phrase about putting his holy Spirit within him may refer to the tradition in Numbers 11 about God giving some of the spirit of Moses to the seventy (two) elders. The purpose of that incident (even though it does not seem to have been followed up!) was to assist Moses in the proper administration of the people, i.e., it had a function that included morality and respect for God. The phrase in Isaiah may therefore be an interpretation of the Numbers

[111] C. Westermann, *Das Buch Jesaiah, 40-66*, (Das Alte Testament Deutsch), Göttingen: Vandenhoeck & Ruprecht, 1966, pp. 305-307.

tradition that gives it a dimension that is not explicit in the Numbers passage.

(h) Isaiah 11.2

> The Spirit of the LORD shall rest upon him:
> the Spirit of wisdom and understanding,
> the Spirit of counsel and might,
> the Spirit of knowledge and of the fear of the LORD.

This verse describes the king who, according to verse 1, will come from the stock of Jesse, i.e. of the line of David. He is the ideal hoped-for ruler. The Spirit of the Lord will rest upon him, presumably as a result of his being anointed at his coronation. The translation of the Hebrew construction which is rendered by 'of' in the traditional renderings has been discussed above. The passage can be paraphrased as follows: the Spirit that makes possible wisdom and understanding, etc. This is not an invasion from outside of the king of a power that imposes something that was not there before. It is an enhancement of latent potentialities within the king, made possible among other things by the office which he occupies, and the traditional expectations or conventions that are associated with it. These are spelled out in the following verses and include fairness in justice, protection of the poor and the meek, and due punishment of the wicked. What these verses tell us about the Spirit of God is that God actively desires justice, compassion, and righteousness, and seeks to achieve these ends through human agencies, especially those associated with distinctive and powerful offices. The Spirit rests upon the ideal king not for his own sake, but for the sake of God's people, and through that people for all the nations.

Conclusion

The use of the term 'Spirit/spirit' in the Old Testament is sophisticated and wide-ranging. It describes a set of human emotions, aspects of character, and intellectual and artistic capabilities. It is the source of life, whether of the created universe or of the lives of human beings. It is the means by which God achieves his purposes through the workings of nature, the inspiring and equipping of leaders, and the unfolding of historical events. It has a dark side, which can make it afflict and mislead leaders and prophets, and turn God from being a friend to being an enemy. It is in this regard an expression of God's sovereignty, and a refusal to be conformed to human expectations. It indicates a God who is certainly on the inside of his creation; and that God's Spirit has a dark side is well summed in Quick's notion of the 'compresence' of God, a presence that both redeems and judges. It is a pity that so much previous scholarship has looked for only 'primitive' aspects of the Spirit in the Old Testament. In fact, it has much to teach us about the Spirit.

CHAPTER 10

The Holy Spirit and the Church Today

I have long felt that the most unhelpful Collect of those in the Book of Common Prayer is that for the Sunday after the Ascension.

> O God, the King of Glory, who hast exalted thine only Son Jesus Christ with great triumph unto thy Kingdom in heaven: We beseech thee, leave us not comfortless; but send to us thy Holy Ghost to comfort us, and exalt us unto the same place whither our Saviour Christ is gone before.

While it is true that the Collect draws upon biblical ideas, for example, the promise of Jesus in John 14.18 'I will not leave you comfortless: I will come to you' it creates a rather unfortunate impression. I am reminded of a dog waiting anxiously outside a shop for the re-appearance of its owner. The Collect seems to envisage a Real Absence of God until Whitsunday; and the function of the Holy Spirit, when he comes, seems to be limited to comforting believers, and helping them to be ready to leave this world for a better one. There is no sense of the Spirit empowering the Church to proclaim the gospel; and even the Collect for Whitsunday is more concerned with 'right judgement' (whatever that is) and comfort than with mission. If I am right in arguing that for many churchgoers the 'gap' between the ascended Jesus and their experience of God is filled by a Holy Spirit restricted to liturgical ceremonies such as Baptism, Confirmation and Ordination, or to 'signs and wonders', it is little wonder that the doctrine and, more importantly, the work of the Holy Spirit is so little understood.

The previous chapters have tried to indicate the enormous variety of language and conceptuality applied to the Spirit of God in the Bible. I shall not attempt to summarise these results. Rather, the present chapter will address a number of practical issues in Christian belief and life, bearing in mind what has been discussed in the earlier chapters. Each topic will come under a sub-heading, and will in some cases repeat what has already been said.

The indwelling of the Holy Spirit
Some biblical language, and much language in prayers and hymns, implies that the Holy Spirit dwells in believers. Paul, at Romans 8.11, writes 'if the Spirit of him that raised up Jesus from the dead dwell in you, he that raised up Christ from the dead shall also quicken your mortal bodies by his Spirit that dwelleth in you'. A prayer has the following words:

O spirit of God, sanctify us wholly:
that in spirit, soul and body we may become thy temple.
Dwell within us and be our God,
and we will be thy servants.[112]

The hymn 'Come down O love divine' has the words

For none can guess its grace,
Till he become the place
Wherein the Holy Spirit makes his dwelling.

What does this language mean, and how are we to under-stand it?

The passage from Romans 8.11 alludes to the creation story in Genesis 2.7, where God breathes the breath of life (*nishmat hayyim*) into the man moulded from the earth, and to the Hebrew idea that it is God's Spirit that makes the difference between life and non-life (Ezekiel 37.9-10). According to this thought-background, the raising of Jesus to new life was the work of God's Spirit. If humans are to experience life beyond life in this world, this must also be the work of God's Spirit who, according to Paul's belief, has been granted to believers as a guarantee, or first instalment of their salvation (2 Corinthians 1.22). The language of prayers and hymns has no doubt been influenced by the biblical language; but it has to be seriously questioned whether such language is helpful for believers today.

---

[112] *New Every Morning*, p. 112.

For Paul, the matter was probably fairly simple. If the difference between a dead person and a living person was that the latter breathed, i.e. had God's spirit (with a small s), the difference between a non-believer and a believer was that the latter possessed God's Spirit (with a capital S). Paul, who was necessarily ignorant of modern physiology and psychology, would have had no difficulty in supposing that God's Spirit in some way existed within a believer, just as the spirit that was the sign of physical life existed within a living person. For us today, language about the Spirit of God dwelling within us must surely be metaphorical. How can we understand it?

We need to think about ways in which we can be inspired, and how inspiration comes to us. It is usually something that comes from outside of us – music, art, literature, sporting events. Something latent within us responds to the external stimulus, and we can be moved to think and do things we might not otherwise attempt. In the religious sphere it will be the same. Preaching, worship, Bible reading, and above all the acceptance at the deepest levels of our being of the fact that God is for us in Jesus Christ may have not only a temporary, but a permanent effect upon the way we understand ourselves and the lives we live in the world. And it cannot be emphasised too strongly that if and when this occurs, we are not filled with some kind of spiritual power, but rather that we gain a new awareness of God. This new awareness may be empowering, but its source is in the awareness of God as *personal*. For the Holy Spirit to 'dwell' in us, therefore, means that we have an awareness of God; and this God is the God and Father of Jesus, whose active presence in the world and our lives we attribute to the Holy Spirit. We need to learn to translate language about the indwelling of a power into language about the presence of a person, a presence that can be a transforming presence.

The gift of the Holy Spirit
in baptism, confirmation and ordination

Here, the difficulty lies in the word 'gift'. A gift is something that someone gives to someone else. The implication is that the gift is subordinate to the giver. It would not be possible for a person to give more than he or she possessed. In the case of the Holy Spirit, the fact that we and liturgies speak of the gift of the Holy Spirit almost carries the assumption that the Holy Spirit is *less* than the person (priest or bishop or elder) who is doing the giving. But if the Holy Spirit is God in action, how can he be 'given' by any human functionary? If there is any 'giving' it must surely be self-giving on the part of God, with human office-holders having the role of publicly affirming God's self-giving.

Ordination is best thought of in terms of what was written about Isaiah 11.2 above. To be ordained is to be admitted to an office that is defined by particular duties and conventions. The purpose of this office is to further the work of God in a particular way. The fact that the office exists means that God has already provided for the exercise of its duties. Through these duties and conventions the latent gifts of the office-holder will be stimulated and strengthened. An ordination service ought ideally to emphasise the teaching in John 15.16:

> Ye have not choosen me, but I have chosen you, and ordained you, that ye should go and bring forth fruit, and that your fruit should remain.

In ordination, the 'giving' of the Spirit means that God pledges himself in a special way to those he has chosen to occupy a special office. It is important here also to emphasise that every Christian has a ministry, not just those who are called to the office(s) of ordination.

Baptism is a different case because infants (I am assuming that baptism means the baptising of infants) are the passive recipients of God's grace, are not aware at the time of God's self-giving, and probably remember nothing of the ceremony in later life. There is also the considerable likelihood that in today's post-Christian world, the baptism will be for the child's family a secular occasion rather than something that marks a desire to bring up the child with a knowledge of the Bible and Christian teaching.

What does it mean, then, to pray that in baptism, God will give his Holy Spirit to the infant?[113] It must be a prayer that God will pledge himself to the child who, in the service, is declared to be not simply the offspring of its parents, but to be a child of God for whom Christ died. Will this make any difference, and does it mean that God will do more for a baptised child than for an unbaptised one? We cannot say; but it may help in a general way if we have a sound conviction that God is at work in the world through his Spirit in ways we cannot know or understand.

Confirmation seems to be an endangered species in today's church. It goes without saying that the idea, seriously voiced in church circles fifty years ago, that Confirmation would

---

[113] See the prayer in the *Book of Common Prayer* beginning 'Almighty and everlasting God, heavenly Father, we give thee humble thanks…'

help young people to cope with adolescence (what was implied was the growing sexual self-awareness of young people) is to be rejected as a crass form of the idea of the Holy Spirit as some kind of infused power. If Confirmation is treated as the adult acceptance of what was done on the person's behalf at baptism, then the stress should be on helping those being confirmed to know about, and respond to, God's commitment that was made to them at baptism. If Confirmation is thought of as a form of adult commissioning to Christian service, then what has been written above about ordination can be suitably adjusted to the lay situation.

Speaking in tongues and other spiritual gifts

From time to time in the course of the history of the church there have been spectacular outbursts of pentecostal phenomena. The most common of the phenomena is 'speaking in tongues' but it has often been claimed that miraculous healings have also occurred. Early in the Nineteenth Century pentecostal phenomena occurring in Port Glasgow preceded a similar outbreak in the church of Edward Irving.[114] In 1994 the Toronto Airport Vineyard Church was the scene of the beginning of the so-called 'Toronto Blessing' in which there was not only speaking in tongues, but people being 'slain in the Spirit' as a result of which they made animal-like noises such as barking and growling.[115]

Such occurrences can be deeply divisive. On the one hand, people can change their ecclesiastical allegiance overnight in order to attend a church that is a place of pentecostal phe-

---

[114] See Flegg, *Gathered among Apostles*, pp. 48-53.

[115] See M. Percy, *The Toronto Blessing*, Oxford: Latimer House, 1996; L. Pietersen (ed.), *The Mark of the Spirit? A Charismatic Critique of the Toronto Blessing*, Carlisle: Paternoster Press, 1998.

nomena. On the other hand, congregations can split, with members who dislike or are disturbed by the phenomena seeking refuge in non-charismatic churches. People's attitudes to the pentecostal phenomena can also be deeply divided. There are those who will see in them true signs that God is at work in power in a particular congregation. At the other extreme the traditional view of the Plymouth Brethren was that such phenomena were intended only for the generation of the first apostles, and that any later appearance of the phenomena was the work of Satan, seeking to lead the church astray.

It does not lie within my competence to assess the validity of pentecostal phenomena. The chapter will proceed by way of some anecdotes which may or may not be helpful. I have certainly heard people speaking in tongues as well as congregations praying in tongues, although such things are not part of my own Christian experience. A doctoral student of mine who lodged at my house, and whose parents had emigrated from Sweden to Canada to establish Pentecostal churches there, once told me that she prayed in tongues every day; and I had no reason to disbelieve her.

While I was at theological college one of my fellow students had been an Elim minister for many years, and was now seeking ordination in the Church of England. Because the Elim church was a pentecostal church, and because the subject interested me, I had a number of conversations with him on the matter of speaking in tongues. He was convinced of the genuineness of the phenomenon, but agreed that members of the pentecostal churches could feel themselves to be under pressure to speak in tongues, even if this was not spontaneous for them. The problem was that unless they did so, the sign was lacking that they had been baptised in the Holy Spirit. They were therefore not fully Christian without the sign. The result was that for some members of these churches the speaking in tongues was simulated, and the danger was created that there was a gulf between simulated (i.e. pretended) spiritual experience and actual experience. This could lead to nervous breakdowns.

Personally I am unhappy about any form of Christian spirituality that lays stress upon achievements as proof of Christian discipleship. I dislike the kind of preaching that seeks to undermine the confidence of believers in an attempt to urge them to greater efforts. I do not endorse complacency, but believe that positive preaching about God's ability to cope with our acknowledged weaknesses can lead to deeper levels of committed discipleship. Without in any way wishing to criticise or denigrate churches where speaking in tongues is regarded as important, I must record my dissent from two ideas that are often implicit in such churches: first, that God's Spirit is present and active only where spiritual gifts are visibly manifested; second, that true and full Christianity is inseparable from the presence of spiritual gifts.

It will be clear from what has already been written in this book that to speak of spiritual gifts is to regard the Holy Spirit as more of a *power* than a *person*, and that I object to this. What God gives is himself, in and through what we call his Spirit. From this perspective, speaking in tongues makes sense theologically only if it is one of the ways in which God assures worshippers of his unmerited mercy and grace, and enables them to respond to him in ways that transcend the use of ordinary human speech. Any implication that this is the *only* form of communion with God that is genuine, and that without it God is not present and active, is quite unacceptable.

Apart from speaking in tongues, the other most common spiritual gift is that of healing. If we confine the discussion to physical, as opposed to mental or spiritual healing, I have no doubt that there are occasions on which God heals people either in connection with prayer, or through the ministry of specially gifted people. The important thing to recognise is that such things depend upon the mercy of God working within the constraints of evil, and are in no way under human control. Some years ago a member of a charismatic house church whom I know, and whose intellectual integrity I respect, was asked to write an article about healings brought about by the exercise of spiritual gifts. She was unable to write the article because she was unable to find any first-hand evidence of such healings. Reports at second hand never produced people who had actually been healed. This does not mean, of course, that spiritual healings through the exercise of spiritual gifts do not occur, but it may mean that their occurrence is exaggerated. There is also the theological point, relevant to any form of Christian healing, that the healing should not be separated from the will and presence of God. Paul's word must never be forgotten, when his prayer for freedom from his 'thorn in the flesh' was 'unanswered':

> My grace is sufficient for thee: for my strength is made perfect in weakness. (2 Corinthians 12.9)

Recovering the Holy Spirit

It is sometimes said that God is about to bring a great revival to the church, by pouring out his Spirit. I have two difficulties with such forecasts. First, they presume that the Holy Spirit is not at present active in the church, or is active in only a very limited way, and I wonder how we can know this. Second, it is assumed that when the revival comes it will take spectacular forms, including manifestations of spiritual gifts. Of course, no one is in a position to know in what form God may choose to bring about revival, if he does, so it would be wrong to deny that it might take the form of spectacular manifestations of gifts of the Spirit. What concerns me is that implicit in such thinking is the idea of the Holy Spirit as power rather than as person. Power is a notion that can easily be corrupted to conform to human ideas of power, in terms of large numbers of people and spectacular events. Yet, as the chapter on Jesus and the Holy Spirit showed, Jesus conducted his own ministry in simplicity and obscurity, and Paul was more concerned to boast about his failures than his successes. There is surely far too much in the teaching of Jesus about the first being last and the greatest being the least to sanction the idea that the values of the Kingdom of God must be identical with the values of our as-yet-not fully-redeemed world, so that any great revival will have to display what is humanly called 'success'. The marks of the Holy Spirit are those described in Galatians 5.22: love, joy, peace, patience, kindliness, goodness, faithfulness, gentleness, self-control. If only some of these marks are present to a small degree in a congregation, God's Spirit is at work there. Moreover, if the Holy Spirit is God, present and active in the world, then wherever the Word of God is preached and the sacraments are duly administered, the Holy Spirit is present.

Congregations need to be encouraged to believe that God is on the inside of his creation, that he is compresent in the world and the church, however unlikely this may seem. To try to achieve this small aim may be to enable God to bring revival to his church, whatever form this may take.

BIBLIOGRAPHY

P.R. Ackroyd, *The First Book of Samuel* (Cambridge Bible Commentary), Cambridge: Cambridge University Press, 1971

C.K. Barrett, *The Holy Spirit and the Gospel Tradition*, London: SPCK, 1966 (new edition)

C.K. Barrett, *The Epistle to the Romans* (Black's New Testament Commentaries), London: A. & C. Black, 1962

C.K. Barrett, *The First Epistle to the Corinthians* (Black's New Testament Commentaries), London: A. & C. Black, 1968

C.K. Barrett, *The Second Epistle to the Corinthians* (Black's New Testament Commentaries), London: A. & C. Black, 1973

C.K. Barrett, *The Acts of the Apostles* (International Critical Commentary), vol.1 Acts I – XIV, Edinburgh: T. & T. Clark, 1994

F. Brown, S.R. Driver, C.A. Briggs, *A Hebrew and English Lexicon of the Old Testament*, Oxford: Clarendon Press, 1906

R. Bultmann, *Theologie des Neuen Testaments*, Tübingen: Mohr Siebeck, 1984 (9th ed.)

E.D.W. Burton, *The Epistle to the Galatians* (International Critical Commentaty), Edinburgh: T & T. Clark, 1921

A. Clutton-Brock, 'Spiritual Experience' and 'Spirit and Matter' in B. H. Streeter (ed.), *The Spirit, God and his relation to man considered from the standpoint of Philosophy, Psychology and Art*, London: Macmillan, 1919, pp.279-309, 312-346

A.B. Davidson, *Hebrew Syntax*, Edinburgh: T.& T.Clark, 1901 (3rd. ed.)

M. DeRoche, 'The *ruah elohim* in Gen 1.2c: Creation or Chaos?' in L. Eslinger and G. Taylor, *Ascribe to the Lord. Biblical & other studies in memory of Peter C. Craigie*, Sheffield: JSOT Press, 1988, pp.303-318

W. Dietrich, C. Link, *Die Dunklen Seiten Gottes*, vol.2. *Allmacht und Ohnmacht*, Neukirchen-Vluyn: Neukirchener Verlag, 2000

W. Dietrich, *Samuel* (Biblischer Kommentar Altes Testament VIII), Neukirchen-Vluyn: Neukirchener Verlag, 2010

C.H. Dodd, *The Johannine Epistles* (The Moffatt New Testament Commentary), London: Hodder and Stoughton, 1946

S.R. Driver, *Notes on the Hebrew Text and the Topography of the Books of Samuel*, Oxford: Clarendon Press 1913 (2nd ed.)

B. Duhm, *Das Buch Jesaia*, Göttingen: Vandenhoeck & Ruprescht, 1922 (4th ed.)

C.W. Emmet, 'The Psychology of Grace: How God Helps' in Streeter, *The Spirit*, pp.159-195

L. Eslinger, G. Taylor (eds.) *Ascribe to the Lord, Biblical and other studies in memory of Peter C. Craigie*, Sheffield: Sheffield Academic Press, 1988

J.A. Fitzmyer, *The Gospel according to Luke I-IX* (The Anchor Bible), New Haven: Yale University Press, 1970

C.G. Flegg, *'Gathered Under Apostles' A Study of the Catholic Apostolic Church*, Oxford: Clarendon Press, 1992

G. Fohrer, *Geschichte der israelitischen Religion*, Berlin: de Gruyter, 1969; English Translation, *History of Israelite Religion*, London: SPCK, 1973

J. Fuerst, *A Hebrew and Chaldee Lexicon to the Old Testament*, (trans. S. Davidson,) London; Williams and Norgate, 1867 (3rd ed.)

J.W. Gibbs, *A Hebrew and English Lexicon to the Old Testament… from the German Works of Gesenius*, London: Howell and Stewart, 1837

K. Gloy, 'Schellings Naturphilosophie. Grundzüge und Kritik' in R. Hiltscher, S. Klinger (eds.), *Friedrich Wilhelm Joseph Schelling* (Neue Wege der Forschung), Darmstadt: Wissenschaftliche Buchgesellschaft, 2012

J. Gnilka, *Das Evangelium nach Markus* (Evangelisch-Katholischer Kommentar zum Neuen Testament II/1), Zürich: Benzinger Verlag, 1998 (5th ed.)

G.B. Gray, *The Book of Isaiah* (International Critical Commentaty), I – XXVII, Edinburgh: T.& T. Clark, 1912

R. Hempelmann, 'Zungenrede II' in *Theologische Realenzyklopädie*, 36, Berlin: de Gruyter, 2004, pp.764-5

J. Héring, *La première épitre de Saint Paul aux Corinthiens* (Commentaire du Nouveau Testament), Neuchatel: Delachaux & Niestlé, 1959 (2nd ed.)

T. **Holtz**, *Die Offenbarung des Johannes* (Das Neue Testament Deutsch), Göttingen: Vandenhoeck & Ruprecht, 2008

A.R. Johnson, *The Vitality of the Individual in the Thought of Ancient Israel*, Cardiff: University of Wales Press, 1964 (2nd ed.)

L.E. Keck, 'The Spirit and the Dove' *New Testament Studies* 17 (1970/71), pp.41-67

J.N.D. Kelly, *Early Christian Doctrines*, London: A. & C. Black, 1958

A.T. Lincoln, *Ephesians* (Word Bible Commentary), Dallas: Word Books, 1990

A.T. Lincoln, *The Gospel According to St. John* (Black's New Testament Commentaries), London: Continuum, 2005

N. Lohfink, 'Charisma. Von der Last der Propheten' in *Unserer großen Wörter. Das Alte Testament zu Themen dieser Jahre*, Freiburg: Herder Verlag, 1977, pp.241-251

E. Lohse, *Die Texte aus Qumran*, Munich: Kösel Verlag, 1964

U. Luz, *Das Evangelium nach Matthäus* (Evangelisch-Katholischer Kommentar zum Neuen Testament 1/ 2 3), Zürich: Benzinger Verlag; Neukirchen-Vluyn: Neukirchener Verlag, 1996 (2nd ed.)

C. Markschies, 'Montanismus' in *Religion in Geschichte und Gegenwart 4*, Tübingen: Mohr Siebeck, vol. 5 pp. 1471-2

J. Monod, *Zufall und Notwendigkeit, Philosphische Fragen der modernen Biologie*, Munich, 1971

New Every Morning, London: British Broadcasting Corporation, 1936

E.A. Nida, *Toward a Science of Translating, with Special Reference to Principles and Procedures involved in Biblical Translating*, Leiden: E.J. Brill, 1964

M. Noth, *Das vierte Buch Mose: Numeri* (Das Alte Testament Deutsch), Göttingen: Vandenhoeck & Ruprecht, 1966

W. Pannenberg, *Systematische Theologie*, Band 1, Göttingen: Vandenhoeck & Ruprecht, 1988

M. Percy, *The Toronto Blessing*, Oxford: Latimer House, 1996

L. Pietersen (ed.), *The Mark of the Spirit? A Charismatic Critique of the Toronto Blessing*, Carlisle: Paternoster Press, 1998

F. Proctor, W. H. Frere, *A New History of The Book of Common Prayer. With a Rationale of its Offices*, London: Macmillan, 1905 (3rd ed.)

O.C. Quick, *Catholic and Protestant Elements in Christianity*, London: Longmans, Green and Co., 1924

O.C. Quick, *Doctrines of the Creed. Their Basis in Scripture and Their Meaning Today*, London: Nisbet & Co., 1938

H.W. Robinson, *The Christian Experience of the Holy Spirit*, London: Collins, Fontana Books, 1962

J.A.T. Robinson, *The Body. A Study in Pauline Theology*, London: SCM Press, 1957

J.W. Rogerson, *Old Testament Criticism in the Nineteenth Century. England and Germany*, London: SPCK, 1984

J.W. Rogerson, 'Can a Doctrine of Providence be based on the Old Testament?' in L. Eslinger, G. Taylor (eds.) *Ascribe to the Lord, Biblical and other studies in memory of Peter C. Craigie*, Sheffield: Sheffield Academic Press, 1988, pp. 529-43

J.W. Rogerson, 'Zechariah' in J. D. G. Dunn, J. W. Rogerson (eds.) *Eerdmans Commentary on the Bible*, Grand Rapids: Eerdmans, 2003, pp. 721-9

J.W. Rogerson, *A Theology of the Old Testament. Cultural Memory, communication and being human*, London: SPCK, 2009

J.W. Rogerson, *The Art of Biblical Prayer*, London: SPCK, 2011

H.P. Schütt, 'Person' in *Religion in Geschichte und Gegenwart 4*, Tübingen: Mohr Siebeck. vol. 6, 2003, p.1120

H. Seebass, *Numeri* (Biblischer Kommentar Altes Testament IV/2), Neukirchen-Vluyn: Neukirchener Verlag, 2003

N.H. Snaith, *The Distinctive Ideas of the Old Testament*, London: Epworth Press, 1944

H.L. Strack, P. Billerbeck, *Kommentar zum Neuen Testament aus Talmud und Midrasch*, Munich: C.H. Beck, vol. 1, 1926

B.H. Streeter (ed.), *The Spirit, God and his relation to man considered from the standpoint of Philosophy, Psychology and Art*, London: Macmillan, 1919

J.V. Taylor, *The Go-Between God. The Holy Spirit and the Christian Mission*, London: SCM Press, 1972

E.E. Urbach, *Hazal-Pirqe emunoth vedeot*, Jerusalem: Magnes Press, 1971, (Hebrew); English Translation, *The Sages : Their Concepts and Beliefs*, Jerusalem: Magnes Press, 1975

G. Vermes, *The Complete Dead Sea Scrolls in English*, London: Allen Lane, 1997

C. Westermann, *Das Buch Jesaiah, 40-66* (Das Alte Testament Deutsch), Göttingen: Vandenhoeck & Ruprecht, 1966

INDEX OF BIBLICAL REFERENCES

INDEX OF PERSONS & SUBJECTS

THE AUTHOR

J W Rogerson

John William Rogerson was born in London in 1935 and educated at Bec School, Tooting, the Joint Services School for Linguists, Coulsdon Common, where he completed an intensive course in Russian, and the Universities of Manchester, Oxford and Jerusalem, where he studied theology and Semitic languages. He was ordained in 1964 and served as Assistant Curate at St. Oswald's, Durham. From 1964 to 1975 he was Lecturer, and from 1975 to 1979 Senior Lecturer in Theology at Durham University before moving in 1979 to become Professor and Head of the Department of Biblical Studies at the University of Sheffield, retiring in 1996. He was made an honorary Canon of Sheffield Cathedral in 1982 and an Emeritus Canon in 1995. In addition to many essays and scholarly articles, his published books include *Myth in Old Testament Interpretation* (1974), *Psalms* (Cambridge Bible Commentary, with J. W. McKay, 1977), *Anthropology and the Old Testament* (1978), *Old Testament Criticism in the Nineteenth Century: England and Germany* (1984), *The New Atlas of the Bible* (1985, translated into nine languages), *W. M. L. de Wette. Founder of Modern Biblical Criticism. An Intellectual Biography* (1991), *The Bible and Criticism in Victorian Britain. Profiles of F. D. Maurice and William Robertson Smith* (1995), *An Introduction to the Bible* (1999, 3rd edition 2012), *Theory and Practice in Old Testament Ethics* (2004), *According to the Scriptures? The Challenge of using the Bible in Social, Moral and Political Questions* (2007), *A Theology of the Old Testament. Cultural memory, communication and being human* (2009), *The Art of Biblical Prayer* (2011). He was awarded the degree of Doctor of Divinity for published work by the University of Manchester in 1975, and has also been awarded the Honorary Degree of Doctor of Divinity by the University of Aberdeen and the Honorary Degree of Dr. theol. by the Friedrich-Schiller-Universität, Jena and the Albert-Ludwigs-Universität, Freiburg im Breisgau.